You will be filled with awe as y[...] ated the authenticity of the autl[...] offensiveness and diminishing efl[...] [...] and the power of God's life-giving grace. I believe that it will strengthen many.

— **Alex Afriyie**, Senior Pastor, London Network Church, London

David Cassidy, a trusted leader with extensive pastoral and international experience, is adept at working across denominational lines and with diverse evangelical leaders. He has much to say that will be of profit to many people, no matter their background or their standing in relation to Christ.

— **Al Barth**, Vice President and Global Catalyst, Redeemer City to City

What a refreshing book! . . . *Indispensable* is just that—both indispensable and a treasure. It reminds Christians about what is really important (and we need to be reminded about) and allows searchers to see the essence of the Christian faith clearly. Read this book and give it to your friends. You and they will rise up and call the author blessed.

— **Steve Brown**, Author; *How to Talk So People Will Listen*; Founder, Key Life Network

This really is classic Reformed theology at its very best. And [it's] all . . . presented with the humility, grace, and personal charm that is the trademark of David's preaching. Though structured around Christian basics, his book will challenge and delight you wherever you are in your spiritual journey.

— **Ray Cannata**, Senior Pastor, Redeemer Presbyterian Church, New Orleans; Coauthor, *Rooted: The Apostles' Creed*

David Cassidy is unique; he's simply not like most pastors. . . . He is well traveled, widely read, smart, and a magician in the kitchen— and the melding of those ingredients, together with a heavy diet of adversity, has produced a man who can serve a feast of wisdom. That wisdom is lavishly offered in *Indispensable*—which, simply put, is rich nourishment for the soul.

　　—**Ray Cortese**, Pastor, Seven Rivers Presbyterian Church, Lecanto, Florida

David Cassidy's book . . . brings compelling clarity in a confusing time. It delivers the core of Christianity, wrapped in interesting anecdotes and poignant stories from the author's own life. . . . *Indispensible* helps to tell the best possible story—the true story that is the last hope of a lost world.

　　—**Nancy French**, Coauthor of *God's Double Agent* and *For the Right Reasons*

A good apologist is first and foremost a faithful witness. In this remarkable book, David Cassidy acknowledges that knowing good arguments is not enough. Instead he has listened carefully to the questions that nag at all of our hearts and minds, and he offers testimony of how he himself has found substantive, sound, and satisfying answers. Highly recommended.

　　—**George Grant**, Author, *The American Patriot's Handbook*; Pastor, Parish Presbyterian Church, Franklin, Tennessee

What a great resource! *Indispensable* offers brief but colorful and compelling explanations of essential truths such as union with Christ, the purpose of the sacraments, the necessity of the body, and the reality of suffering in the life of a believer—the kinds of topics that are usually reserved for longer theological tomes that most ordinary believers simply won't read.

　　—**Nancy Guthrie**, Bible Teacher; Author, *Seeing Jesus*

Through the years I have observed David Cassidy to be both brilliant and pastoral—a rare and enviable combination. His insights consistently take me somewhere I would not otherwise have gone. . . . Whenever he speaks, I am all ears. . . . This is the kind of book that we want folks to read at our church. It is real. It is raw. It is honest. It offers Jesus. And it is beautiful.

—**Mike Khandjian**, Pastor, Chapelgate Presbyterian Church, Marriottsville, Maryland; Author, *A Sometimes Stumbling Life*

David has the rare ability to take profound biblical truths and apply them to my life. In *Indispensable*, he teaches me that the fundamentals of the Christian faith are absolutely necessary as I walk through the trials, sorrows, and challenges of life. . . . David winsomely portrays God's indispensable truths in the life and fabric of the church. I heartily recommend this book.

—**Jay Kyle**, Vice President of Asia Pacific and Latin America, Redeemer City to City

This book serves as both an excellent introduction to Christianity for those outside the kingdom of God and a warm reminder of what's truly indispensable about our faith for those who already know and worship Jesus. A deeply encouraging book.

—**Eric Landry**, Senior Pastor, Redeemer Presbyterian Church, Austin, Texas; Executive Editor, *Modern Reformation* Magazine

If, like me, you have no time for optional frills but are open to the classical Christianity through which millions have found reality with God, this book will satisfy you. I wish everyone . . . would read this book!

—**Ray Ortlund**, President, Renewal Ministries; Council Member, The Gospel Coalition

I am thankful for David Cassidy's pastoral ministry and for this book, which holds high the essentials of the Christian faith and does so in a way that presents Scripture as both important and inviting.

—**Russ Ramsey**, Pastor, Christ Presbyterian Church, Cool Springs location, Franklin, Tennessee; Author, Retelling the Story Series

What an amazing labor of love by my friend, David Cassidy! This scholar-pastor has written a systematic theology that informs the mind, stirs the heart, and guides the will. Whether you are a professional theologian, a seasoned pastor, an engaged layperson, or a searching unbeliever, this book will bless you.

—**George Robertson**, Senior Pastor, Second Presbyterian Church, Memphis, Tennessee

Among the handful of books I regularly share with new Christians and with those who are exploring the Christian faith, *Indispensable* is poised to become a compelling, trustworthy go-to. . . . I highly recommend that you not only read *Indispensable* but also share it liberally with others.

—**Scott Sauls**, Senior Pastor, Christ Presbyterian Church, Nashville; Author, *Befriend* and *Irresistible Faith*

A gifted speaker reveals that he is a gifted writer—with a superb turn of phrase and accessible language at every turn. His writing is littered with quotable nuggets. As it says on the cover, this book is truly *Indispensable*.

—**Daniel Singleton**, Editor, *Faith With Its Sleeves Rolled Up*; National Executive Director, FaithAction

David Cassidy spells out what is indispensable to the Christian life, reminding us in every chapter that the truth of Christ is not an answer to a question. It's an entirely new way of being—a new life. This is an ideal book for those who are just starting on the way—who want to know what they believe—and for all those interested in helping anyone in that pursuit.

—**Rankin Wilbourne**, Lead Pastor, Pacific Crossroads Church, Los Angeles; Author, *Union with Christ*

INDISPENSABLE

INDISPENSABLE

THE
BASICS
OF
CHRISTIAN
BELIEF

DAVID P. CASSIDY

P&R

P U B L I S H I N G

P.O. BOX 817 • PHILLIPSBURG • NEW JERSEY 08865-0817

Unless otherwise indicated, Scripture quotations are from the NEW AMERICAN STANDARD BIBLE®. Copyright © 1960, 1962, 1963, 1968, 1971, 1972, 1973, 1975, 1977, 1995 by The Lockman Foundation. Used by permission.

Scripture quotations marked (CEV) are from the Contemporary English Version Copyright © 1991, 1992, 1995 by American Bible Society. Used by Permission.

Scripture quotations marked (ESV) are from the ESV® Bible (The Holy Bible, English Standard Version®), copyright © 2001 by Crossway, a publishing ministry of Good News Publishers. Used by permission. All rights reserved.

Scripture quotations marked (NIV) are taken from the Holy Bible, New International Version®, NIV®. Copyright © 1973, 1978, 1984, 2011 by Biblica, Inc.™ Used by permission of Zondervan. All rights reserved worldwide. www.zondervan.com The "NIV" and "New International Version" are trademarks registered in the United States Patent and Trademark Office by Biblica, Inc.™

Scripture quotations marked (NKJV) taken from the New King James Version®. Copyright © 1982 by Thomas Nelson. Used by permission. All rights reserved.

Italics within Scripture quotations indicate emphasis added.

Excerpt from "The Wasteland" from *Collected Poems 1909–1962* by T. S. Eliot. Copyright 1936 by Houghton Mifflin Harcourt Publishing Company. Copyright © renewed 1964 by Thomas Stearns Eliot. Reprinted by permission of Houghton Mifflin Harcourt Publishing Company. All rights reserved.

Printed in the United States of America

Library of Congress Cataloging-in-Publication Data

Names: Cassidy, David P., author.
Title: Indispensable : the basics of Christian belief / David P. Cassidy.
Description: Phillipsburg : P&R Publishing, 2019.
Identifiers: LCCN 2018050054| ISBN 9781629954264 (pbk.) | ISBN 9781629954271 (epub) | ISBN 9781629954288 (mobi)
Subjects: LCSH: Theology, Doctrinal--Popular works.
Classification: LCC BT77 .C244 2019 | DDC 230--dc23
LC record available at https://lccn.loc.gov/2018050054

For "T":
beautiful, brave, and bold.

I believe in Christianity as I believe that the Sun has risen, not only because I see it, but because by it I see everything else.
—C. S. Lewis, The Weight of Glory

Grant me, O Lord my God, a mind to know you, a heart to seek you, wisdom to find you, conduct pleasing to you, faithful perseverance in waiting for you, and a hope of finally embracing you. Amen.
—Prayer of Thomas Aquinas

CONTENTS

FOREWORD

David Cassidy and I met in downtown Franklin, Tennessee, over twenty-five years ago at the four-corner intersection of gospel beauty, Spirit renewal, compassionate orthodoxy, and robust worship. My young church family was riding the waves of a wonderful work of God, and David could taste redemptive salt-spray all the way up in Paducah, Kentucky. He came to see for himself what was going on.

Not long after my first cup of coffee and heart-engaging chat with him, a total stranger became a treasured friend. And in a twist that neither of us could have ever anticipated, David was called to be my successor as senior pastor of Christ Community Church in Franklin. This story brings me happy tears and incredible joy every time I tell it.

Now, this is a foreword for David's new book—not a toast or, thankfully, his eulogy. And I would offer a glowing endorsement of *Indispensable* even if I didn't know and love David. But I *do* know him, and I can't separate his heart from his art. I enjoy a ringside seat as the contents of this book are being lived out right in front of me, in a community and city that I love.

What do I love most about David's new book? First of all, the title simply rocks. I have longed for a just-the-right-size book to give to non-believers and believers alike—one that would cut to the redemptive chase and present the heartbeat of Christian belief in a concise, inviting, and intelligent manner. *Indispensable* is that book. I don't want a book called *Exhaustive*, because it'd be too big and expensive, and I wouldn't trust any author who claimed such expertise.

You will find *Indispensable* perfect for reading with neighbors or friends who are interested in exploring why we refer to the gospel of Jesus Christ as good news. It's also a great book to use in discipling relationships with believers at any level of spiritual maturity.

Second, I love the focus and contents of *Indispensable*. As someone who loves to travel, David has surveyed the vast geography of God's grace and culled thirteen topics that represent the Alps of Christian belief. I'm sure he debated long and hard before settling on these thirteen chapters—but he chose wisely. If anything, this overview of gospel spirituality simply makes me hungry for my friend's next book.

Third, I love the taste and aroma that fills all thirteen of these chapters. As a gifted chef, my friend knows how to combine the right spices, heat, and time for whatever dish he's preparing, for the culinary enjoyment of those who gather around his table. *Indispensable* isn't just a book of truth. It's a banquet of beauty. It invites all of us to taste and see that the Lord is good.

It's one thing to fill a shopping cart with the right ingredients, but it's quite another to combine them in a way that is welcoming, nourishing, and satisfying for others. This is why I mentioned that I can't separate David's art from his heart. As I read each chapter of *Indispensable*, I hear David's room-filling laugh, I feel the fire of his convictions, I enjoy the breadth of his Renaissance-man learning, and I am convicted by the God-smitten heart that beats in his chest.

But above all, this book makes Jesus more beautiful, God's grace more accessible, and the gospel more *indispensable* to me.

Scotty Smith

ACKNOWLEDGMENTS

There's a lot of interweb noise these days about "self-publishing"—but surely that's as inaccurate a description of the process of book writing, printing, and distribution as might be imagined. The number, for instance, of people who were involved in this little project, as well as their giftedness, really is quite significant, and it would be very unbecoming to fail to note their contributions.

This book wouldn't have happened were it not for my Texas friend Steve Webb, who first contacted me about doing a project for P&R. I also have to thank the good people at P&R for taking the risk of helping me to develop and publish this book, noting most especially the remarkable editorial skills of Amanda Martin, the "vocabulary whisperer." She brought my "power words" into harness with her skillful hand and made this work presentable and understandable. Thank you, Amanda! I also have to mention my gifted and dedicated assistant, Tyler Bingham, who patiently combed through the manuscript and chased down countless citations. She was preceded in that work by my friend Neil Andrews, who, together with Diana Batarseh, handled the song-lyric copyright issues.

That was tedious work—but Neil and Diana always brought immense joy and a careful eye to the process. My thanks as well to Wes Garner for chasing down some of the particularly elusive citations.

In some ways, preaching is an act of thinking aloud—an always dangerous practice!—and so I have to thank the gracious congregations in Great Britain, Kentucky, Texas, and Tennessee for their patience with me in the ministry as, over the years, I preached through the issues that ultimately led to this book. The members of the churches I've served have always taught me more about the gospel and the faith than I ever taught them, inspiring me and allowing me the space and time to explore the riches of Scripture. They were first on the scene to rejoice whenever in the course of that work I got to yell, "Eureka!" Without those congregations this book would never be a reality, because they have always been the only people I was trying to serve. My one purpose has always been simply to labor at building up churches in faith, hope, and love. The chapters here are the result of my care for them, offered now with hopes for their continued benefit as well as for that of a wider readership.

Thank you to my colleagues Ken Leggett and Charles Johnson, who, together with the aforementioned Diana, reviewed the manuscript and offered valuable corrections, insights, and suggestions for clarification. Thank you as well to the session and diaconate of Christ Community Church for allowing me the time to work on this project—you know how very much I love you all and how grateful I am for the privilege of serving with you.

The debt that I owe my dad and mom is manifold, and this is especially true in regard to this book. Mom taught me to read. Then Dad taught me to read C. S. Lewis via *The Screwtape Letters*. Both taught me the basics of Christianity—not simply by what they said but by the way they lived. My mother has already finished her journey, and my dad still runs his race right here—I'm glad we will all share eternity together and that you loved well and long a deeply flawed son.

Most of all, thanks to Toni for her wisdom, faith, love, constant encouragement, and indispensable devotion to Jesus and his mission.

Every one of the people above has been utterly *indispensable* to the writing of this book. I am your grateful debtor.

Finally, thanks be to God, for from him and through him and to him are all things. To him be glory forever. If anyone at all is helped by the words I have written, it can only be because God is merciful and kind. He is the God who condescends to draw straight lines with crooked sticks—who is always doing deep things in human hearts that make us all exclaim, "Only God could have done that!"

INTRODUCTION

The Indispensable Presence

Christianity . . . , if false, is of no importance, and,
if true, of infinite importance. The one thing it
cannot be is moderately important.
—C. S. Lewis, God in the Dock

I will be with you.
—Jesus Christ

A few years ago, I met a Russian Christian named Alexander Ogorodnikov—a dissident during the years of the persecution that was inflicted on Christians by the Soviet Communist state. He was in Cambridge to lecture, and, together with some friends, we talked late into the night. What he shared with us is something that we all need to hear.

Alexander had been imprisoned in Siberia for his faith. On one particularly grim night in the prison, the guards had isolated him, stripped him, broken the windows of his cell, and turned off all heat. They expected the Siberian night to do their work for them and kill him. Freezing and alone, Alexander felt the prayers of other Christians come over the walls and down the hall to the cell where the guards had left him. "These prayers surrounded me and warmed me," he said. "In the morning, expecting me to be dead, the guards found me not only alive but well and warm. God was with me through the prayers of his people."

God was with me.

What an astonishing statement. I wonder if we believe that is still possible. Do we have faith that God will be near to us and real to us in this age of advancing technology and declining love and intimacy? Do we know what it means to be a Christian, to have faith, and to persevere in that faith in the face of pain and disappointment? I ask these questions because many of the Christians I meet hold to a strange imposter of the faith—a substitute for the Savior himself. The gods of success and accumulation and pleasure are center-stage, even in the churches—a message of baptized self-salvation that guarantees prosperity and freedom from all troubles, rather than a true sufficiency found in Jesus himself and a faith that holds on more tenaciously than the problems that seek to undo it.

I ask these questions because they are questions I have wrestled with, too. The Christian ministry has brought me face-to-face with the worst pains and nightmares that we fear. During my years in the pastorate, I have helped to clean up after suicides, sat with a grief-stricken man and woman whose five-year-old grandson had just drowned in their pool, watched a two-year-old battle cancer and lose the fight, and buried my wife's best friend, who was killed in a horrifying auto accident. I have given up the baby I was in the process of adopting, because the birth mother changed her mind (which was always her right). I've watched my wife struggle with a disease that is known to kill and paralyze. I could mention many more instances of grievous human suffering—more than enough to counterbalance whatever joys I have seen as well.

In addition, I have faced the private horror of my own sins and wondered about the authenticity of my own feeble faith. Others have seen and experienced far worse suffering; but for my part, I have seen enough to make me question God's care for me, for those I love . . . and frankly for our entire sin-soaked world, which drips in blood from violence and cries in pain from hunger and neglect. We appear to be immersed in a culture that loves death, worships mere celebrity, seeks power at all costs, and will stoop to everything from torturing animals to honoring animal instincts with the status of virtue. God with us? Really?

During one especially dark time, my wife was dying, as far as anyone could tell, and I had no real reason to hope she would recover. Even if she did, our lives would be forever altered. The old doubts and questions rushed in as I cried into my coffee in a hospital cafeteria in Austin, Texas. I needed some air . . . and a better cup of coffee.

Heading out the door, I saw something I hadn't noticed on the way in: the door to the chapel. I went in and, directly in front of me, saw a small crucifix—a cross with Jesus hanging on it in agony. The cross. The crucified. Frankly, that's the only God who I find credible and even beautiful, and he's the one who keeps meeting me in those dark places. The crucified God. Do you ever think about him?

If I am to have faith at all, it will never be in some absentee God or some pitiably weak cosmic "invisible friend"—not in some impersonal force or fate, but in a God who knows our suffering because he made it his own.

"IT IS FINISHED!"

At the heart of the Christian message are the explosive words Jesus uttered as he died on a Roman cross in the first century. "It is finished!" he exclaimed (John 19:30)—and at those words the earth shook, time as we know it split in two, and the relationship between God and people changed forever.

In essence, "It is finished" was Jesus's own declaration that the debt his people owed for their treason against God had been completely satisfied by his perfect life and sacrificial death. Their debt was paid in full. In his love for us, he paid the penalty that we couldn't possibly discharge. He lived the life that we should have lived but couldn't and died the death that we deserved to die but didn't. Those words and that cross, a symbol of fear and horror to ancient people, became the Good News—indeed the best news that anyone had ever heard. "God was in Christ reconciling the world to Himself, not counting their trespasses against them," Paul would later write (2 Cor. 5:19). The sign of fear became the emblem of hope, and the words of a dying man were a life-giving announcement from God himself.

How could this be? Because after uttering those words as he hung on a cross on a Friday afternoon, Jesus rose from the dead on Sunday morning. Jesus's resurrection wasn't merely God's exclamation point on Jesus's words, or even the vindication of Jesus and his suffering. In the resurrection, God announced the defeat of death and the grave; he liberated people who through the fear of death had been living as slaves; he reversed the curse of the catastrophe that had befallen and bedeviled the human race and the planet and entire cosmos.

Because of what Jesus did on Friday afternoon and what happened to him on Sunday morning, we can be certain that our sins are forgiven, that we are beloved of God, that our hope for the eternal future is secure, and that our world, broken and bruised by the wounds we inflicted on it, will be healed and restored. This is the indispensable heart of Christianity.

"IT IS DONE!"

That ultimate recovery of everything that has been lost, the healing of everything that is now broken, is at the core of Jesus's words at the end of history, recorded in Revelation. "It is done!" Jesus cries (Rev. 21:6), putting the final touches on redemptive history and bringing to a bright and brilliant conclusion the loving work he undertook so long ago. It's the ultimate Hollywood ending: the Champion vanquishes evil and gets the gal. The church is his bride, and we are invited to the "marriage banquet" to live in the celebratory love of our Savior for all eternity. In Tim Keller's words, it's the day when through "the Gospel, because it is a true story . . . all the best stories will be proved, in the ultimate sense, true."[1]

INDISPENSABLE CHRISTIANITY: LIVING IN THE SPACE BETWEEN

We live in the space between "It is finished" and "It is done." What God has finished through Jesus's death and resurrection, and will bring to culmination in the coming kingdom of Jesus, is cause for immeasurable joy and thanks. We have faith in what God accomplished on the day Jesus cried, "It is finished." We also have faith that the day will come

---

1. Timothy Keller, *Hidden Christmas: The Surprising Truth Behind the Birth of Christ* (New York: Viking, 2016), 28.

when we hear Jesus say, "It is done." What we have to figure out is how to live by faith in between those two days—in the space between the *now* of "It is finished" and the *not yet* of "It is done." We live in the meantime—and it's an awfully mean time at times.

Given our place in this story, the question that was asked so well by Francis Schaeffer arises: "How should we then live?" How do we live here and now in the light of gospel promise and gospel hope? After all, so much pain surrounds us, and our world groans under the weight of tremendous injustice. Poverty remains unchecked in much of the world; weapons of mass destruction may be unleashed; disease and plague prey on many; the planet itself is undergoing significant shifts that affect people and animals of all kinds. Violence fills the streets and screens. Chaos and tragedy befall all. Earthquakes and tsunamis swallow cities. Sexual violence and confusion abound. Opiate addiction and suicide are on the increase. Christians are beheaded and crucified by Islamic extremists. Advances in science inevitably raise challenging issues, from pursuing "designer children" and abortion to extending a life when the body and brain seem to be past their expiration dates. We find ourselves baffled by questions that seem unanswerable.

We see our children abandoning the faith that prayerful parents sought to nurture in their souls. We see marriages of many years unexpectedly dissolving and once-full churches emptying out. We see charlatan preachers offering magic cures and quick fixes that seduce the unguarded and produce in many others a jaundiced cynicism about the church. We see the places that we expected to be shelters in the storm turned into harbors where dangerous men with dark hearts prey on vulnerable children.

When we look within, we see our own legions of lust,

fear, greed, anger, and despair still standing strong at the gates of our minds—and calling for reinforcements.

How do we live in such a time as this?

"I AM WITH YOU ALWAYS"

In point of fact, as vexing as this is, the situation these days is no different than it has ever been. Violence and warfare, poverty and disease, persecution and perversion, hypocrisy and hype have marred our world since the human story began. The church has endured challenge for two thousand years, and it will continue to do so. In fact, it has faced these threats and welcomed them, discovering through its martyrs the courage of resilient faith. Along its often difficult journey, the church has, in its better days, embraced the call to care for the weak and sick and, through its educational endeavors, offered light to drive back the darkness of ignorance and fear. The church has reclaimed areas that it once lost. Even when it is displaced in one region, it continues to expand in others.

How should we then live? Perhaps the question can arise from a more hopeful place. A heart-changing experience of Christ's powerful presence in our lives is essential for us in the meantime. By this I don't mean a light-hearted, jovial approach to the faith that smiles and says nothing in the face of trials or that chooses to dance when weeping is called for. What I do mean is a living awareness of the nearness of Jesus in our deepest trial and sorrow, of his grace for us in our great need, of his strength that matches our well-known weakness. It means that we live with the awareness that he is with us in all places and at all times. That's especially true when we may not have a sense of his nearness.

Think of Joseph, the son of Jacob, whose dream led to the deliverance of so many people—including his own brothers, who treated him with such treachery. Joseph waited so long for his vision to be fulfilled. "The LORD was with Joseph," the Scriptures say (Gen. 39:2) as they record his years of rejection, imprisonment, and humiliation. God was with him!

Or consider the friends of Daniel, who were thrown by King Nebuchadnezzar into the flames of a furnace in Babylon for their refusal to bow down and worship an idol (see Dan. 3). Peering into the conflagration, the king saw not only the three men whose deaths he'd ordered alive and well, but also another presence who was walking with them in the flames.

Between "It is finished" and "It is done," we live, Peter tells us, as exile people—as those who are on a journey to our home and are living that journey before the eyes of others (see 1 Peter 2:11–12). And on the journey, God is with us.

The great poet T. S. Eliot was not unfamiliar with despair and painful loss. He also knew that, as we go through life's bitter struggles and challenges, we are not alone. Recounting the terrors that befell the members of Shackleton's expedition to the Antarctic and their recorded experience of an unaccounted-for companion as they trudged through the howling wind, Eliot wrote,

> Who is the third who walks always beside you?
> When I count, there are only you and I together
> But when I look ahead up the white road
> There is always another one walking beside you
> Gliding wrapt in a brown mantle, hooded
> I do not know whether a man or a woman
> —But who is that on the other side of you?[2]

2. T. S. Eliot, "The Waste Land," in *Collected Poems: 1909–1962* (New York: Harcourt Brace & Company, 1964), 67.

We have a long road ahead, personally and collectively. We have suffering to endure and doubts to be overcome. We have difficult questions to answer and difficult seasons ahead for whole nations, churches, and families. Disease will make its presence felt. Doubts will crowd in. Death will lurk close at hand. Cultural collapse in the West shows no signs of abating—the winds will blow; the rain will beat down; the floods will rise. One cannot help but think that there is, in James Taylor's words, more "fire and rain" on the horizon.

Will the house stand? That all depends, as Jesus said, on whether or not we build our lives on the truth of his Word and commit our lives to that Word as the path we will travel (see Matt. 7:24–27). If we do, then the experience of Eliot will belong to others, too. As they see us walking in the Way, they too will note the presence of another. Nothing then could be more indispensable than a vibrant and deeply rooted Christian faith. We first start to make this faith our own by turning our gaze on the wonder of the one who promises to be Immanuel—God with us.

1

JESUS CHRIST

The Indispensable Answer

*Somebody as intelligent as Jesus would've been
an atheist if he had known what we know today.*
—Richard Dawkins, interview with The Guardian

At the name of Jesus every knee should bow.
—Paul the Apostle

Without money and arms, [he] conquered more millions than Alexander, Caesar, Mohammed, and Napoleon; without science and learning, he shed more light on things human and divine than all philosophers and scholars combined; without the eloquence of schools, he spoke such words of life as were never spoken before or since, and produced effects which lie beyond the reach of any orator or poet; without writing a single line, he set more pens in motion, and furnished themes for more sermons, orations, discussions, learned volumes, works of art, and sweet songs of praise, than the whole army of great men of ancient and modern times.[1]

Everybody has an opinion on Jesus. He's unavoidable. He's so wise and good that even those who don't confess the faith that he taught want him on their team. What do you make of Jesus?

Jesus of Nazareth burst onto the scene around AD 30 in Roman Judea, a small nation dominated by a foreign power and its puppet king. The Jews of Judea were a remnant who lived mostly in and around Jerusalem but were also scattered in considerable numbers across the first-century Mediterranean world. Despite many divisions within their community, they held a shared hope: that one day a deliverer would arise to rescue them from their enemies and reunite them in God's kingdom. They called that person *Messiah—Christ*, in Greek.

How did Jesus come to be regarded as that promised Messiah by a great many of the Jews, and later by millions more who were convinced by that very Jewish message about him? How did this man who marshaled no army, was executed as a criminal, and wrote nothing but a few unrecorded words in the dirt come to be regarded as the Savior of mankind?

Many men had sought to claim to be the Messiah, but no one had fulfilled the ancient hope in the eyes of the multitudes. No one, that is, until Jesus came to preach in their cities and towns. The people encountered him as one of their own—a neighbor, an extraordinary and mystifying figure who created peace and tension, who brought profound threat as well as profound relief. They didn't see him at first as God or even as the Messiah. They didn't see him through the eyes

---

1. Philip Schaff, *The Person of Christ: The Miracle of History* (New York, 1866), 48–49.

of the church or through the eyes of history. They did see him as a teacher with unspeakable wisdom. They saw him as a visionary who spoke of "seeing" the kingdom of God and of what it meant to live in that kingdom.

But they also saw something more. Jesus had the power to perform miracles, and that took things to a different level. They knew that through their long-expected Messiah, as he had with Moses and Elijah long beforehand, God would return with signs and wonders to save his people. So, when the people heard Jesus and saw the miracles that he performed, they started asking one supreme, astonished, and sometimes indignant question: *"Who is this?"*

"Who is this, who even forgives sins?" (Luke 7:49 ESV)

"Who is this? Even the wind and the waves obey him!" (Mark 4:41 NIV)

The whole city was stirred and asked, "Who is this?" (Matt. 21:10 NIV)

Who indeed!

"Who do you say that I am?" Jesus asked (Matt. 16:15). How we answer determines our destiny, just as it determined the destinies of those who first heard the question so long ago.

TAKING JESUS SERIOUSLY

We must start with Jesus, because without him there is no Christianity. The truth of Christianity rests on the reality of his identity. If Jesus is who the Scriptures claim, then your decision whether to follow or ignore him carries the greatest possible consequences for life—now and forever. In the same way, if the claims that he made about himself and that others made about him are false, then Christianity is of no more consequence than a religion that worships doorknobs. Doorknobs can at least open doors—whereas dead men whose words are lies, no matter how lovely they are, are not much good for anything at all.

Huston Smith, one of the greatest scholars of comparative religion in our time, wrote that only two religious figures in human history were so utterly different from everyone else, so completely set apart, that people asked them, *"What* are you?" Those two are the Buddha and Jesus. Buddha answered, "I am awake" and continued to direct his disciples to look away from him. Jesus answered, "I am the Way," instructed his disciples to fix their eyes on him, and received their worship.[2] No mere man would do such a thing, especially a Jewish man within the cultural context of Jewish monotheism that reverenced God and his worship in emphatic, even violent terms. Jesus is nothing like others who claimed to be a Messiah— and there were many. He appears on the scene as an entirely different kind of person. In the category of religious leaders in history, Jesus is utterly unique.

The uniqueness of Jesus is vital to grasp from the start. There has never been anyone else like him. "The great Russian philosopher Nikolai Berdyaev said that a wind of freedom blows through [Jesus's] teachings that frightens the world and makes us want to deflect them by postponement— not yet, not yet! H. G. Wells was evidently right: Either there was something mad about this man, or our hearts are still too small for his message."[3]

2. See Huston Smith, *The World's Religions: Our Great Wisdom Traditions*, rev. ed. (New York: HarperCollins, 1991), 82.

3. Smith, 326.

Don't dismiss Jesus with faint praise, calling him a great teacher or reducing him to a messenger who is no more divine than any other religious leader. Those whose hearts have been captured by Jesus would sacrifice everything in order to pursue what Paul called "the surpassing worth of knowing Christ Jesus my Lord" (Phil. 3:8 NIV). Even if you choose to reject Jesus, it's important that you recognize the truth about him and reject *that*, rather than rejecting a mythical Jesus who bears no resemblance to reality.

Singer-songwriter Leonard Cohen wrote, "Any guy who says 'Blessed are the poor. Blessed are the meek' has got to be a figure of unparalleled generosity and insight and madness . . . a generosity that would overthrow the world if it was embraced because nothing would weather that compassion."[4] And, in fact, ultimately the world of the first century didn't weather Jesus's compassion. It rejected Jesus's message of mercy, nailed him to a cross, and killed him.

We shouldn't lose sight of the fact that Jesus was put to death because he was a political threat to the powers of his time. Whoever Jesus was, he was not a "nice" person spouting lofty platitudes about peace; no, Jesus was a threat, despite his goodness—or, rather, precisely because of his goodness. Jesus was good but was considered as good as dead by his opponents, both religious and secular, because he was everything they weren't and the people knew it. For those leaders, it was "Jesus or me," not "Jesus for me"!

To the religious leaders of his day, Jesus was a dangerous radical, upsetting the temple establishment and creating the kind of social upheaval that would invite the ruling Romans to send in soldiers to slaughter the crowds, close the temple,

4. Jim Devlin, *Leonard Cohen: In His Own Words* (London: Omnibus Press, 1998), 58.

and possibly destroy Jerusalem. For them, it was better that Jesus be killed rather than countless others; it was better that Jesus be stripped of his public adulation before they lost their positions and authority. And it would be unwise for us to ignore their concerns. As Jesus's contemporaries and those who were responsible in some ways for the good order of large numbers of people, these religious leaders have to be taken seriously if we want a robust view of Jesus.

There can be little doubt that Jesus was radical, and deeply so—a person who subverted the accepted order of his time. The question then is whether the religious leaders' concerns about him were valid. In certain ways, they were. Jesus's rising popularity would have caught the attention of the Roman occupying forces, and they may well have seen in him the risk of a popular revolt. They were not likely to permit that situation to develop. Jesus's followers wrote that false accusations were made about him, sometimes out of jealousy. Given his sudden popularity and the size of the crowds that he drew, that is completely believable. The significant factor that undermines fears about him, however, is that Jesus never sought to lead a political movement or incite a violent uprising. Far from it. The idea that Jesus was a *dangerous* radical falls on the grounds that his enemies underestimated how radical he really was. They feared a military leader; Jesus said, "Put your sword away."

To tackle the important matter of Jesus's identity, it only makes sense to turn to his closest contemporaries: his earliest followers.

WHAT PETER SAID: THE ANOINTED ONE

We all know what it's like when a teacher asks a question that his or her students realize is tricky. They hesitate; they hedge; they know that the teacher has an answer in mind, and they don't want to appear foolish.

"Who do you say that I am?" When Jesus asked that question, the same thing happened with his disciples. At first, they ventured the opinions of others. "Well, Jesus, some people say . . ."—finishing this with some colorful possibilities: Elijah, Jeremiah, John the Baptist back from the dead. Then suddenly, from the back of the class, one of Jesus's very first disciples gave a robust and unflinching reply. "You are the Christ, the Son of the living God" (Matt. 16:16).

Peter's reply wasn't the result of a Sherlock Holmes moment. His insight was God-given. "Flesh and blood has not revealed this to you, but my Father who is in heaven," Jesus told him (v. 17 ESV). God had showed Peter Jesus's true identity as the long-expected Christ. His answer not only brings a deep and hidden mystery to the light but also shows us the starting point for answering Jesus's question ourselves.

While many people might think of "Christ" as something like Jesus's last name, the word *Christ* is more a title than a name. It means "the anointed"—a phrase that shows up repeatedly in the Old Testament. Kings were anointed, as were prophets and priests. Israel's Messiah was the sum of all three: *the* King, *the* Prophet, and *the* High Priest. As King, Christ protects and governs his people; as Prophet, he brings God's truth through his Word; as a faithful High Priest, he makes us right with God by offering up his life on our behalf once for all and by constantly interceding for us without end. Christ cannot fail to bring to his side and into his eternal city all those for whom he died and rose again—those whom he has awakened by his truth.

In certain ways, Peter's confession of faith was a prophetic insight into what Jesus would accomplish through his mission. Peter didn't base his answer on what had already happened, but instead declared Jesus's identity as a way of saying why he had come to begin with. Peter didn't grasp everything that this entailed, as his subsequent actions show, but his words that day help us understand how to respond appropriately to Jesus right now.

Sometimes we want a partial Jesus—we want Jesus the Priest, who gives his life to forgive us, but we push back against the idea of Jesus the King who governs us. Or we prefer Jesus the truth-teller but have little patience for Jesus's mercy and forgiveness when his truth exposes our falsehood. But Jesus cannot be so divided. You cannot have a Savior who is not also your King. You cannot have a Prophet who is not also your Priest. We have the total Jesus or no Jesus at all. Like Jesus's beautiful, indivisible garment for which Roman soldiers gambled when they crucified him, Jesus himself is an indivisible Lord.

This is a cause of immense joy and comfort when we stop to ponder it. The God of Truth is also the merciful Savior. The Lord of heaven is also our King who, unlike kings who demand that their servants die to protect them, instead dies on behalf of his people in order to deliver them from the forces of darkness. The Savior who dies is the King who rises to reign and to lovingly protect his people, bringing them safely into his kingdom, and who will come again in fiery majesty to extend the scepter of his rule over the entire cosmos, bringing all things into subjection to his love and mercy.

Jesus's miracles brought the people the conviction that they had, at last, found their long-expected Messiah. For, as in the days of Moses and Elijah long beforehand, God was showing up with signs and wonders to save his people.

WHAT JOHN SAID: GOD IN THE FLESH

Not everything that Scripture says about Jesus is meant to be easy, even if it is clear. The task of our faith is not to offer easy answers to difficult questions but often, in fact, to point to mysteries beyond our comprehension.

This is true of the opening of the gospel of John: "In the beginning was the Word, and the Word was with God, and the Word was God . . . and the Word became flesh and dwelt among us" (John 1:1, 14). John uses a word in this passage that was loaded with meaning for the Greco-Roman world: the term *Logos*, which we translate as "Word." Logos was believed to be the supernatural unifying power behind the visible world, and claiming the existence of Logos in the beginning would have affirmed the view of reality that John's readers already held. John goes on, however, and writes of the Logos as "he." That was a stunner. The invisible power behind the visible world was and is God, and God has come to us as Jesus Christ.

This is one of the greatest truths that we must understand about Jesus, difficult to grasp though it may be: while Jesus is 100 percent human, he is also 100 percent God. John writes that God the Word took on flesh—our human nature—so that he might reveal his love and accomplish his saving mission to die for his people. Jesus is the God-Man.

This is what Christmas is all about. Far from the wild unwrapping of presents and the joyful parties and feasts that we associate with the season, Christmas celebrates God's entrance into the world in the most surprising manner. God becomes one of us—a helpless baby, born in filth to a woman in poverty on the margins of the world, far from the corridors of power. Can that be true? Is it really true that Mary's baby boy is also God come in the flesh? That's what John is saying. When we realize that this is the case, we cannot help but bow in wonder with the shepherds and offer our treasures in worship with the magi.

In the face of Jesus, we see the face of God. Jesus was not shy about affirming this. "If you have seen me," said Jesus, "you have seen the Father" (John 14:9 CEV). On several occasions, Jesus used the forbidden phrase "I Am"—God's unfathomable Name that was revealed to Moses—to describe himself. This is all the more shocking when we remember the culture in which these words were said and written. No sane Jewish man—and Jesus was exactly that—would have dared utter such things, knowing that, unless they were true, they were blasphemous. "Before Abraham was, I am" (John 8:58 ESV).

Here is an even greater shock. If Jesus is God become human, then the God who saves us is the serving, loving, sacrificing, humbly zealous person whom we see in Jesus—in Cohen's words, "a figure of unparalleled generosity and insight and madness." What a difference this makes! The Creator of the universe—the God of glory—is the humble God, the helpless God lying in the manger. From his first moments, he was identified with food for the hungry. Born in a stable in Bethlehem, a name that means "House of Bread," Jesus was laid in a food trough, identified from his first moments among us with food—a hint of what was to come when he would one day say that he is the Bread that comes down from heaven and that his flesh is true food. He is the weeping God, the man of sorrows and acquainted with grief, our shepherd in the valley of the shadow of death. He is the God who stoops to wash our feet, the crucified servant God who suffers with us and for us. In the words of Isaiah, "Here is your God!" (Isa. 40:9 NIV). As author Brennan Manning writes, "God entered into our world not with the crushing impact of unbearable glory but in the way of weakness, vulnerability and need."[5]

God the Word becomes flesh—Jesus the Christ, born of Mary—so that he might make God's glory known and win a fallen, broken world back to God. He reconciles the human race in his own body through his conception and birth and through his crucifixion and death. This God, the cross-bearing God, is the one who saves us by sacrificing himself.

The impact of this truth for faith is far-reaching. We Christians face an old dilemma that certain people use as a touchstone for rejecting Christian faith or even theism in a more general sense. It's often called "the problem of pain," and it goes something like this: "You Christians claim that God is both good and powerful—but when we see so much suffering and horror in the world, we have to ask why God, if he's all-powerful, doesn't put a stop to it. Either God is all-powerful and has the capacity to stop all suffering but refuses to put an end to the pain, and is therefore not good; or God is good and would love to put a stop to it but can't, and is consequently not all-powerful. Your God is no god at all—at least not one we can accept—being either powerful but cruel or kind but impotent." The cross of Christ stands as an answer from God to this pointed accusation about his character.

"I could never myself believe in God, if it were not for the cross," wrote John Stott. "In the real world of pain, how could one worship a God who was immune to it?"[6] Stott confesses that the problem of pain, while not satisfied by an answer that human philosophy wants to accept, is overcome in his soul because God—far from standing off in a distant corner

5. Brennan Manning, *The Relentless Tenderness of Jesus* (Grand Rapids: Revell, 2004), 203.

6. John R. W. Stott, *The Cross of Christ*, 20th anniv. ed. (Downers Grove, IL: InterVarsity Press, 2006), 326.

of the universe to observe our pain in either malign indifference or impotent weakness—does indeed intervene and take to himself the full scope of human suffering and injustice at the cross. "God crucified" is the God who makes pain his own and overcomes the great source of all suffering: our decision to be our own gods rather than to trust him as loving Father.

If part of us reads this and exclaims, "How can these things be?" then we are in good company, for that's exactly what Jesus's own mother also said. If part of us grasps this truth and humbly bows in awestruck worship before Jesus, then, along with his disciple Thomas, who said to Jesus, "My Lord and my God!" we are also beginning to see the light, even if we cannot comprehend the why and the how of these things. God, after all, isn't so much the subject of our study as he is the cause of our wonder. Rather than generating formulas for our thinking, he gives shape to our souls.

WHAT PAUL SAID:
SON OF DAVID AND SON OF GOD

In his letter to the Roman Christians, the apostle Paul introduces his message as the gospel of God that reveals Jesus Christ as "a descendant of David according to the flesh, who was declared the Son of God . . . by the resurrection from the dead" (see Rom. 1:1–4). Like John, Paul clearly states that Jesus is fully God and fully man. The Savior of the world is a man, descended from King David, and a divine person as well—the Son of God who conquers death and sin.

Those of us who are familiar with Christian faith may on reflection find it unusual that Paul starts his gospel with a reference to King David. We more often present Jesus as the Son of God, and that is altogether fitting. What is behind Paul's starting with David—Israel's great shepherd-king?

To understand this, we need to know that the promises made about Israel's future Messiah very frequently referred to King David. David was Israel's great warrior-king, who killed Goliath and secured Israel's safety; he was their leader in worship and wrote many of the psalms; he was Israel's great prophet, who spoke through the lyrics of his songs of the future kingdom of God. His dynastic line lasted for hundreds of years, until his people were carried away into exile in Babylon.

God made a promise—a covenant—with David to establish one of his sons on his throne forever. In the years leading up to the exile and the years that followed, prophets like Isaiah, Jeremiah, and Ezekiel reminded the people of God's promise—that God would bring a King to them and, through that King, once again save them from the hand of their enemies. Isaiah foretold of a new and anointed King who would spring from "the root of Jesse," David's father (Isa. 11:10). Jeremiah reiterated the covenant promise that God made to David and foresaw the day when a new "righteous Branch" would spring up for David (Jer. 23:5). Ezekiel prophesied that God would gather his scattered people into one flock and give them a loving shepherd like David (see Ezek. 34:22–24). For many centuries, Israel rightly anticipated that their long-expected Messiah would be the son of David—a new King in that line who would resurrect their hope and fulfill God's promises.

When we turn to the New Testament, we discover that Jesus was born of a descendant of David and was made the legal son of David's line by Joseph, the husband of Mary. Mary and Joseph journeyed to Bethlehem, the City of David, for Jesus's birth. Jesus is frequently hailed as the "Son of David"— the one who would bring mercy to the suffering. At the very outset of his life, the magi from the East were led by the star to seek the one who was "born King of the Jews" (Matt. 2:2). At the very end of his life, Pontius Pilate hung on Jesus's cross a sign indicating the crime for which he was executed: "The King of the Jews," it read—in Latin, Greek, and Aramaic, so that *no one* missed the point (see John 19:19–20)! The tables are turned by the resurrection, and Paul announces to the Romans that Jesus is indeed the King, the Son of David.

We gain two great emphases from this. First, Jesus fulfills the promises that God made to his people. The very first of these promises was made all the way back in Eden, after humankind's uprising against God, which was inspired by the serpent's cunning. God immediately stepped into the disaster and promised that a descendant of the woman would be born to crush the head of the serpent, though in doing so he would suffer the bruising of his heel. The promise given to us right from the start is that our enemy would be defeated by a man whose conquest over the serpent would be complete in its scope but costly in its execution. He would suffer pain, he would be bruised, in order to vanquish this terrible foe. God promised Abraham that, through one of his sons, God would bless the entire world. He promised David that one of his sons would sit on his throne eternally. In Jesus's crucifixion, resurrection, ascension, and coming-again-in-glory, God brings to pass every promise he has made.

Second, Jesus's enthronement at God's right hand indicates that he is the Lord of all persons, places, and things in the entire universe. No aspect of creation is not subject to his authority. When we say, "Jesus is Lord," we mean that there is no higher authority than Christ himself, the Son of David seated on the eternal throne of God, the King of Kings and Lord of Lords.

Having noted Jesus's full humanity, Paul also affirms Jesus's full divinity—he is the "Son of God." As Son of God, he is Mediator between God and humankind, uniting us in himself and bringing us into communion with God. As a man, he arrives through birth, as do we all; as Son of God, he arrives from heaven, as no one else has done or can do. The Holy Spirit's raising Jesus from the dead backs up this outrageous claim, Paul notes.

Peter connected the phrase "Son of God" with Jesus's being the Messiah: "You are the Christ, the Son of the living God" (Matt. 16:16). Paul does much the same thing. The Messiah, the Savior of Israel and the world, must be fully divine in order to deliver us from our tragic condition and to reveal the eternal God. He must also be fully human in order to fulfill God's promises and to satisfy the just demands of God's law on our behalf as our representative.

WHAT WILL YOU SAY?

We can now see a lovely composite sketch of God's Savior—of Jesus—and can more adequately answer the question "Who do you say that I am?"

Taking their cue from these passages, Christians across many cultures through the centuries have answered with one heart and voice, "Jesus is Lord." The followers of Jesus who I noted in this chapter all died for the testimony they gave—sometimes in a very cruel fashion. Tortured and then crucified or beheaded, they sealed the claims that they made with their own blood. They were willing to die in horrific ways because they could not deny what they'd seen and come to understand about Jesus. Their faithful witness should make us sit up and take seriously what they had to say. The way that they answer the question "Who do you say that I am?" should inform the way that we answer.

And how will you answer this question?

"Jesus, you are the Christ, my Messiah. Jesus, you are the God, the Word, come to make the Father known and to bring me into communion with him. Jesus, you are the Son of David—please reign over my life. Jesus, you are the Son of God and the Savior, the only one I can call Lord, the one who has come from heaven and will bring heaven's kingdom here and bring me to the center of that great new civilization."

I hope you can answer that way. Even if you cannot yet do so, I hope you will continue to read along and will discover with me next the indispensable basis for what we believe about Jesus.

When I was once confessing some real doubts about the viability of faith in an age of technology, a kind friend replied, "That's all completely understandable, but what are you going to do with Jesus?" It turns out that Jesus is not only indispensable but also unavoidable! Pop culture tries to reduce Jesus to a celebrity—the kind of iconic figure we see on T-shirts: Elvis, Marilyn, Michael . . . famous people who are so large that only one name is needed to know who we're talking about. Scripture doesn't allow us this option when it comes to Jesus; it will not reduce him to a hero, good man, wise sage, social-justice warrior, cultural icon, or demi-deity to be added to the collection of other dashboard good luck charms. Jesus is not merely your "bestest friend," in the words of Lana Del Rey[7]; as we've seen, he is infinitely more. It's the "more" that we have to wrestle with.

---

7. Lana Del Rey, vocalist, "Body Electric," by Lana Del Rey and Rick Nowells, track 4 on *Paradise*, Interscope Records, 2012.

FOR REFLECTION OR GROUP DISCUSSION

1. In what ways do people end up diminishing the significance of Jesus by sounding as if they are praising him?

2. Many of Jesus's contemporaries rejected him—and ultimately killed him. What was so offensive about him and his teaching?

3. Jesus asked, "Who do you say that I am?" How would you answer him?

4. Peter asserted that Jesus was the Messiah (Christ), the Son of God. What does the Bible mean by the term *Messiah*?

5. John claimed that Jesus was God come in the flesh. Why is this claim so vital to Jesus's mission to save the world?

6. How does the idea of God being revealed as the "suffering God" change your idea of his character?

7. Paul began his message about Jesus by identifying him as "the Son of David." Name two or three ways in which Jesus being the Son of David impacts us now.

8. As a group, sing "Crown Him with Many Crowns" by Matthew Bridges.

2

WORD AND SPIRIT

The Indispensable Source

You must be born from above. . . .
You must be born . . . by the Spirit.
—*Jesus Christ*

Those in whom the Spirit comes to live are God's
new Temple. They are, individually and corporately,
places where heaven and earth meet.
—N. T. Wright, Simply Christian

A wonderful—and probably apocryphal—story about Ernest Hemingway celebrates his undoubted genius. While he was at a lunch with several other authors, one of them bet the great man that he couldn't write a short story in six words or less. Hemingway took the bet, pulled out a pen, and wrote on a napkin: "For sale: baby shoes, never worn."

Stories need not be long to be profound, gripping, and true.

The gospel of John is all those things. It's especially deep and compelling when John records intimate conversations between Jesus and people who wanted to know more about him. One such person was a highly educated member of the ruling class—a man who had a prestigious pedigree and possessed real power. By today's measure, he was Ivy-League smart, Wall-Street wealthy, DC-empowered, and Cathedral-dignified—a member of the culturati. He came to visit Jesus in the dead of night—in all likelihood to protect his social standing from scandal as he sought out this new and controversial religious leader. His name was Nicodemus.

NEW BIRTH[1]

Nicodemus begins by saying, "We know . . ."—and what ensues is a total verbal smackdown from Jesus.

Does that surprise you? As you read the Gospels, you'll soon realize that Jesus does not put up with pride, and especially religious pride, for even a moment. Jesus brushes aside Nicodemus's assertions about what is "known" and goes straight to the heart of the matter: Nicodemus has to start over. He needs to be *born again*—born from above and by the Spirit.

This is a humbling and astounding diagnosis for those whose pedigrees, education, street addresses, and professional accomplishments define their existence. It's easy to think that the people who need a "new birth" are the people who, at least in our view, are . . . well, "needy"—people who don't have much education; people without access to power and wealth; people who can't achieve the kind of success that others envy. Maybe drug addicts. The poor. People in prison. They need a fresh start. But Nicodemus? Us?

1. We read of this encounter in John 3:1–21.

This is the astonishing thing. When Jesus talks about being born from above and by the Spirit, he addresses precisely the person we would least expect. But Nicodemus needs to hear Jesus's words, and the reason for this is pretty simple, really. Nicodemus doesn't know where he is broken, and he doesn't know how broken he truly is. The man who began the conversation by saying, "We know . . ." knows neither the true identity of the person he is speaking to nor the true state of his own life.

"*What?* Born *again?*" Nicodemus's response is predictable. "How can a man get back inside his mother and start over again?"

"You're a leading theologian, and you don't get this?" Jesus asks in response. "These are the basics, and you don't even know them?"

Poor Nicodemus—his pride is being shredded. Because Jesus loves Nicodemus, he won't let him live with the facade of acceptability for even a second more.

"How?" Nicodemus wants to know.

It turns out that Bob Dylan had it right. "The wind," said Jesus. "See the wind blow? There's your answer."

Why would Jesus employ the wind as a way of speaking about the Holy Spirit? To understand that, we need to recall the way that the ancient Hebrew prophets also spoke of the Holy Spirit, along with one of the nuances of their ancient language that we might miss in our English translations. Linguistically, in Greek and Hebrew, *breath* and *wind* and *spirit* go together. That's also true biblically and theologically. When Jesus says, "You must be born of the Spirit" and points Nicodemus to the movement of the wind, he shows him the power and freedom that the Spirit's movement has for bringing new life into being.

Jesus was also reminding him of an old story that

Nicodemus knew very well: the story of the Valley of Dry Bones (see Ezek. 37:1–14). In this account, the Hebrew prophet Ezekiel was shown a grim vision of a desert valley floor filled with the scattered bones of Israel's dead soldiers.

"Can these bones live?" God asked the prophet.

"Only you know, Lord," was the prophet's wise reply.

God instructed Ezekiel to preach to the bones (an apt description of what a lot of pastors face every Sunday). When he did this, the bones rattled and jumped—then began to find each other and join together. Flesh formed on the skeletons, but there was no life in them. Now Ezekiel was looking at a valley of corpses.

"Prophesy to the wind," God told Ezekiel next. That is, he was to speak to the Spirit and summon him to the scene. The roar of the Spirit's arrival filled the valley, and the breath of God came into the corpses; they jumped up, moved into formation, and stood at attention, resurrected by God's Spirit through God's Word as uttered by a prophet.

WHAT NICODEMUS NOW KNEW

Jesus cut Nicodemus down to size. This very accomplished man moved from a place of self-assured prestige to a place of deep awareness of his authentic situation. Like the dry bones in Ezekiel's vision, Nicodemus was a dead man with no hope apart from the wind blowing into his life and lungs. He needed resurrection; he needed to be born of the Spirit.

In chapter 1, I asked how you would answer Jesus's question "Who do you say that I am?" Nicodemus also asked, "How?" How was new birth possible?

Jesus's answer is still true today: "You must be born again . . . by the Spirit." Everything that Nicodemus imagined would commend him to God was, in fact, a barrier. My friend, it's not just "crazy, wild" sins and failures that create barriers between us and God but our "religious sins," our self-salvation projects, our misguided, mismanaged attempts to offer up to God a "good" life that will somehow lead to his accepting or rewarding us. Eternal life is not a reward for the morally perfect. It's a gift freely given to the broken.

Another major religious leader who needed to learn the "Nic at Night" lesson was from Nicodemus's same social sphere—a man named Saul of Tarsus. Highly trained, and acclaimed as a rising star in theological and religious circles, he was zealous in persecuting the Christian church, which he held to be a deceptive sect. He had an unblemished record of public righteousness and an unimpeachable family pedigree. Yet he came to count all this as "loss" and to lay it aside, noting that he too had to be brought to God by God on the basis of God's grace, not by his own efforts (see Phil. 3:8–9). Despite his religious, academic, and professional accolades, his internal life was marked by darkness. "Nothing good dwells in me," he confessed in his letter to the Roman Christians (Rom. 7:18).

The light broke through Saul's own cracks when, in a scene reimagined in countless works of art, Jesus appeared to him on the road to Damascus, striking him blind so that his eyes could be opened to Jesus's love for him. Saul became a different man that day—born from above by the Spirit's sovereign and gracious work in his life.

WINDBORNE

Saul the zealous persecutor became Paul the pioneer apostle. In his writings, he often speaks of the Spirit's work—of the way in which the breath of heaven enters our lungs and gives us life. In Paul's first letter to the church at Corinth, he wrote of the Spirit being the agent by which God justifies us in his sight (see 1 Cor. 6:11). In his little letter to the Ephesian Christians, he said that the Spirit came to dwell in us and to be the guarantee that what God has begun in us by new birth he will ultimately finish in our resurrection (see Eph. 1:13–14). In his letter to the Galatians, he outlined the characteristic "fruit" of a life that is marked by the Spirit's pervasive influence (see Gal. 5:22–23). In his epic epistle to the Romans, he mentioned the Spirit over and over again, especially emphasizing that by the Spirit—who lives within believers—we are made the adopted sons of God and given all the privileges of such a relationship (see Rom. 8:14–17); moreover, the Spirit in us is the same Spirit that was with Jesus as well (see v. 11).

Dead people can't raise themselves, and babies can't conceive themselves or give birth to themselves. There are many "how to" books on birth for moms and dads, but there isn't one for babies! At the end of the day, the Spirit—the wind— blows where he wishes and hovers over the hearts of his choosing. Faith in Jesus is a gift of the Spirit, as Paul wrote to the Corinthians (see 1 Cor. 12:9).

The Holy Spirit may well be moving in your life right now. You may perceive only a gentle breeze beginning to rise rather than a mighty, rushing, hurricane-force gale, but the velocity isn't the issue. If he is choosing to move in your life, to bring light to cracked and broken places, then God is lovingly drawing you to himself.

Maybe, like Nicodemus, you didn't know that you needed to be born by the Spirit. Maybe you thought that "born again" talk was for people in some kind of desperate need. Well, it is. We each must wake up to the most desperate need we all have—to the brokenness that's in every human heart. We'll look into this more in the next chapter.

THE WIND IN THE WORD

Late in his life, not long before he died a martyr's death at the hands of Roman authorities, Paul wrote to his trusted young protégé, Timothy. Amid other instructions, he told Timothy to work especially hard at studying Scripture. "Study," he wrote, "so that you can handle with accuracy the word of truth" (see 2 Tim. 2:15). Paul knew that Timothy's spiritual health, and the wellbeing of the church in his day, depended on Timothy's study and subsequent teaching of Scripture. Why that emphasis? Why do our lives depend on the Scriptures being studied and faithfully taught?

Paul had a very high view of the Bible. Many people today do not. Yet Jesus himself shared Paul's view. In Matthew's gospel, Jesus asks some of his opponents, "Have you not read what was spoken to you by God?" and then quotes from the Old Testament book of Exodus (see Matt. 22:31–32). In this encounter, Jesus says that a section of the Bible (which was, at that time, over a thousand years old) was spoken by God "to you"—to people living a thousand years after the words had been first recorded. In Jesus's view, reading Scripture is the same as having God sit in your room and speak directly to you. No wonder we are to read and study Scripture.

Through Scripture, God's voice resounds in every generation. Paul picks up on this as he writes to young Timothy that "all Scripture is breathed out by God" (2 Tim. 3:16 ESV). The Word of God that is Scripture exists because the Spirit of God—the breath of God—breathed those words into the hearts and minds of the writers who penned them and sent them to God's people for all time. When we read the Bible, we read words that are written by human beings—but that find their origin in God's heart rather than in man's mind.

Does our view of the Bible align with the view held

by Jesus? If you have a high opinion of Jesus, you should at least consider his view of the Scripture as you think about its claims on your life and its explanations of how God works to make us his own people.

Paul instructed Timothy to study Scripture and entrusted to him a rich inheritance of truth, which included a high view of Scripture. That's what sustained Paul in great suffering; that's what nourished the church in the centuries after Paul died. Paul, like another ancient rabbi, "set his heart to study . . . do . . . and teach" God's Word (Ezra 7:10 ESV). He was like the psalmist who said that God's words were sweeter than honey and exclaimed, "Oh how I love Your law! It is my meditation all the day" (Ps. 119:97)—or like Jeremiah, another Hebrew prophet, who wrote that God's Word was his food, which he took and ate and which was "a joy and the delight of [his] heart" (Jer. 15:16).

Many people misuse the Bible, turning it into a weapon against others. In *To Kill a Mockingbird*, Miss Maudie wryly observes, "Sometimes the Bible in the hand of one man is worse than a whiskey bottle in the hand of [another]."[2] But the abuse of the Bible should not lead to the disuse of the Bible. God's Word is not a textbook to be mastered but a revelation from the God who masters our hearts. It is not a light to warm us but a blazing fire to consume us. It is not a hammer to throw at others but an ice pick to shatter our coldness. It is not a daily snack but our necessary food. Without it, we die.

Over and over again I've seen the Scriptures penetrate hard hearts and transform lives. If you could meet my friend Charlee, a twenty-something lady in Franklin who is married

---

2. Harper Lee, *To Kill a Mockingbird* (1960; repr., New York: Grand Central Publishing, 1982), 60.

to Sam, you'd know what I mean. Charlee started studying the gospel of John with Jill, one of our wonderful women's ministry leaders, and as she did so she was moved from a place of deep woundedness, isolation, and fear to a place of improbable joy, wholeness, and generosity of life. "I'm a miracle," Charlee said to me the other day. "Yes, you are!" was my immediate response. And she really is. Charlee is living proof that the Holy Spirit, working through God's Word, changes lives. That's the power of the gospel to set people free.

GOD'S TRUTH AND OUR MINDS

The darkness that is so personally and socially pervasive isn't limited to the will. It's not just the emotional or volitional aspects of who we are that are affected by the shadows of death. The intellectual dimension of our personhood is affected as well. Our hearts, will, and thoughts are a shambles, and despite our considerable (or at least occasional) accomplishments with self-control, romance, and logical rigor, we remain in desperate need of new data, new direction, and new power.

God has said, "My thoughts are not your thoughts, neither are your ways my ways. . . . As the heavens are higher than the earth, so are my ways higher than your ways and my thoughts than your thoughts" (Isa. 55:8–9 ESV). If God had left it there, this assessment of the situation would not have been especially helpful. What follows makes all the difference. "As the rain and the snow come down from heaven and . . . water the earth, making it bring forth and sprout, giving seed to the sower and bread to the eater, so shall my word be that goes out from my mouth" (vv. 10–11 ESV).

God has not left us in the dark about who he is and what he desires for us. His Word comes down like rain and snow to the drought-stricken soil of our existence, bridging the intellectual and moral chasm between limited, broken humans and the unlimited, all-knowing, all-loving Creator. God speaks our language, communicating his heart and mind in words that we can understand. That's a gift that leaves us gasping in wonder. In Scripture we have access to God's mind. We can't let that sit on the shelf and ignore it!

THE HOLY SPIRIT AND YOU

We've looked at the fact that human beings, while beautiful, are also broken in such a way that only God can mend us. In chapter 1, we saw that God has done so by sending the Light into our darkness: Jesus Christ, who brings healing and wholeness. We've also learned that what happened two thousand years ago in history is applied to us now, personally, through the work of the Holy Spirit, who does this especially through the words of Scripture. So, if the Spirit is working through the Word to make Jesus beautiful and believable to our wounded souls, and if we are given new lives, what does this actually look like?

It's not that we're going to gain "competency" in religious matters; in fact, Christian faith creates an increasing awareness of *incompetency*. No one can be an expert on God. But the questions are worth tackling; after all, we are dealing with infinite things—matters of the eternal. We shouldn't expect easy answers. What we can expect to encounter, and what we really do have, is a loving Guide. Jesus promised that the Holy Spirit would not only give us new life but guide us into all truth as well.

FOR REFLECTION OR GROUP DISCUSSION

1. How would you describe the Holy Spirit and his work?

2. Nicodemus was a person who, in regard to every standard of success in his culture, was on top of the world. He was also deeply religious. Yet he needed a new birth. What are the implications for us of Jesus's words, "You must be born again"?

3. Read Ezekiel 37, about the valley of dry bones. Describe how God's Spirit works to bring new life to those who are lying dead on the floor of the valley.

4. Read Romans 8:11–17 and make a list of (or discuss together) the various ways in which the Holy Spirit works in our lives.

5. What is the relationship between the Spirit of God and the Word of God given in Scripture? Note 2 Timothy 3:16. How does this affect your view of the Bible?

6. Isaiah 55:8–11 acknowledges that with our minds alone we can never know God's will or his ways, but that his Word will be our guide. Do you expect to be guided more by your heart and feelings or by Scripture? Are you looking for new supernatural revelations or are you meditating on and applying Scripture to your life?

7. As a group, sing "Breathe on Me, Breath of God" by Edwin Hatch.

3

BROKENNESS

The Indispensable Admission

Sometimes grace is a ribbon of
mountain air that gets in through the cracks.
— *Anne Lamott,* Grace (Eventually)

In the beginning was the Word . . . and the Word was God . . .
the light. . . . And the Word became flesh and dwelt among us.
—John the Apostle

We live in a time of frequent, loud, and angry protest—
of marchers hoping to make their voices heard when they
believe that those in power are ignoring them. From marches
that assert rights to marches that protest abuses of power, we
see the streets of global cities thronging with thousands of
people who are eager to demand change. Supporters praise
the crowds that gather; detractors criticize their approach
and their cause. We are an aggrieved species—we decry
injustices and hypocrisies and are only too willing to point

them out for all to see . . . as long as they don't incriminate ourselves.

The truth is that we don't like to protest about *ourselves* very much; we would much rather protest the faults of others than confess our own. One of our most clever self-deceptions is that we are largely okay—that our sins aren't as bad as others' are and that God looks down with pleasure on our efforts to right the ship of our souls. But even if we haven't done those things that we condemn in others, we've sure thought about it. We love the sweet taste of revenge, the chaos in people's lives that makes us look more together, and the applause of others—even if we have to do the wrong thing to get it. Our narcissism paralyzes our friendships, dragging everyone we know kicking and screaming back to the common denominator of self: "That's enough about me. Let's talk about you. What do *you* think about me?"

My old childhood pastor put it this way: "If I'm breathing, I'm sinning." Obviously one of our best-practiced sins is covering our tracks—making sure no one sees who we really are. If we were known as we truly are, we would fear being rejected, ostracized, and shamed. We crave being known and loved but can't take the risk of being known truly. If anyone—*anyone!*—knew us truly, they could surely never love us fully. So we hide. Even from ourselves.

Usually it takes some great moment or catastrophe to bring us face-to-face with the faults in our own souls; it takes some deep wound—usually one that we cause another—to wake us up to our own brokenness. We mask our shattered souls fairly well. Professional and academic success, relational fulfillment, physical attractiveness, and fiscal affluence can give the image of invincibility to those who possess those privileges. That's when catastrophe steps in. Disease, death, or divorce; fiscal collapse; betrayal—all the things that make us curse and despair suddenly descend on us without warning . . . and the cracks begin to show. (Or perhaps wonder steps in. Marriage, children, authentic love, and the like can also expose the cracks we have plastered over. Love can hurt.) Both disaster and delight have the power to rip away the facade and break into our self-imposed exile.

LOSING CONTROL

Let me share a secret. God is the great disturber. Many people imagine that God only brings peace, but that simply isn't so. We get comfortable in our routines and perpetuate the lie that we control our existence. God shakes up that self-deceptive way of living all the time. He brings deep disturbance. Something breaks—something that we can't control or fix. Sometimes we can't hide, due to the proximity of people who we love. Our relationships expose the reality we have cleverly hidden away. Events that we couldn't have foreseen expose the untamed and unexplored territories of our interior selves. We keep legions of lusts, fears, jealousies, and anger chained up in the dark basements of our souls, and God unlocks the cellar door as we shout, "No! Leave that one closed! Don't go in there!"

And that's just our own personal lives. We are also part of a culture that loves to hate, that delights in violence, that won't hesitate to spend trillions on wars while resenting every dime that is spent on hunger. We are all too aware of studies that show incredibly high estimates of how much violence young people are exposed to through various forms of media and gaming. We know our police will deal with far too many incidents of domestic and sexual violence—including assaults on children by people who are in positions of trust within medical, ecclesiastical, and other communities that exist to

serve rather than seduce. We turn on our screens and sali-
vate at the prospect of virtual gladiators in combat or smart
bombs taking out our enemies. We dig it . . . and, in doing so,
we dig the grave of our society.

Novelist Flannery O'Connor possessed the remarkable
ability to pull back the thin veneer of acceptable behavior and
expose the darkness underneath. She saw through the masks
that we wear in order to hide from others and conceal our
many faults. As a writer, she knew that we need hope for some
kind of resolution—that what we sense personally is univer-
sally true. Whether the issue is our arrogance, anger, greed,
lust, self-sufficiency, or addictive phobias and substances, we
want those foes vanquished and our broken relationships
healed. She wrote, "There is something in us, as storytellers
and as listeners to stories, that demands the redemptive act,
that demands that what falls at least be offered the chance to
be restored. The reader of today looks for this motion, and
rightly so, but what he has forgotten is the cost of it. His sense
of evil is diluted or lacking altogether, and so he has forgotten the price of restoration. When he reads a novel, he wants
either his senses tormented or his spirits raised. He wants
to be transported, instantly, either to mock damnation or a
mock innocence."[1]

I'm all for protest marches. They even help in some situ-
ations. But where do I go to protest not my innocence but my
inability to deal with my own need for resolution? Where can
I acknowledge that I am part of a species that is addicted to
hatred and violence? Where do I go for a second chance? Where
can I find "the redemptive act"? Is it even available? Maybe the
darkness within and around us is just too deep to undo.

1. Flannery O'Connor, *Mystery and Manners: Occasional Prose, Selected and Edited by Sally and Robert Fitzgerald* (New York: Noonday Press, 1970), 48–49.

The truth is that there is no bargain-basement redemption. There is no easy path to recovering innocence.

DANCING IN THE DARK

Singer-songwriter Leonard Cohen left us a treasury of lyrics and truth that will prove beneficial well beyond the boundaries of his own life. He was personally acquainted with many sorrows, some of which were self-inflicted; he also knew that these points of pain—these "cracks," as he called them—were the places "where the light gets in."[2]

Into the darkness comes the light. Even the Bible opens with the dark. "In the beginning, God created the heavens and the earth. . . . Darkness was over the face of the deep" (Gen. 1:1–2 ESV). That's when the light showed up: "And God said, 'Let there be light'" (v. 3 ESV). We love it when the light shows up to banish the night.

We see this victory in Antoine Fuqua's film *The Magnificent Seven* when Sam Chisholm rides into town to rescue a ravaged population from violence and exploitation. Chisolm arrives dressed in black, contemplating a cross in the burned-out church before leading his unlikely group of mercenaries and forgiven failures into battle for the liberation of everyday people.[3] From the start, we know who's going to win. Whether you prefer the old version with Yul Brynner or the new film with Denzel Washington, the story of light driving out darkness is one that we resonate with down to our little toes. That's how the world is supposed to be. That's what we need: an unexpected champion who comes to our town

2. Leonard Cohen, "Anthem," track 5 on *The Future*, Columbia Records, 1992.

3. See chapter 13 of *The Magnificent Seven*, directed by Antoine Fuqua (2016; Culver City, CA: Sony Pictures Home Entertainment, 2016), DVD.

to free us from the power of one we are too weak to defeat ourselves. We know we can't win, because the enemy, if we care enough to look deeply, dwells within.

Of course, when we recognize our own darkness, we immediately set up some do-it-yourself salvation projects aimed at personal improvement. We set some new goals, decide to do better, and go all "Invictus," shouting, "I am the master of my fate; I am the captain of my soul."[4] The problem is that this isn't going to undo the damage we have already done, or truly alter who we are, or cure our culture.

The *London Times* once ran an essay competition asking its readership to answer the question "What is wrong with the world?" Renowned wit and intellectual G. K. Chesterton wrote back, "Dear Sirs, I am. Yours very sincerely, G. K. Chesterton."[5]

We can't save ourselves if we are the problem that needs to be solved. While we are victims in certain ways, the more radical and unpleasant truth that we seldom like to face is that we are *victimizers* as well—we are the ones who have inflicted pain on ourselves, on others, on creation, and supremely on God himself.

LET'S GET RADICAL

Since 9/11, the word *evil* has regained some popular usage in our culture, and the painfully essential revelations about the abuse of children and women by men with power in religious, business, political, and entertainment spheres

---

4. William Ernest Henley, "Invictus," in *A Book of Verses* (London, 1888), 57.

5. No documentation bears out this story, but the American Chesterton Society has reason to believe it is true. See "What's Wrong with the World?" American Chesterton Society, accessed January 17, 2018, https://www.chesterton.org/wrong-with-world/.

have reinforced our awareness that evil is real and has to be faced. Such language helps us to name an action and begin to deal with it in a just and proper way. The lynching of an African-American man by the Ku Klux Klan, the slaughter of Jews by Nazis, or the sexual abuse of a child is not merely "bad" or even "criminal"—these are examples of evil, and calling them such helps us to censor those who advocate for, defend, or perform such atrocities, while also helping us to arrive at just punishments for these terrible acts. To minimize evil behavior is to diminish justice and give cover to wickedness.

I notice, however, that while *evil* has gone mainstream, *sin* remains a word that is banished to the back of the bus by the culturati. Why do people who don't mind using the word *evil* feel uncomfortable with the word *sin?* I suspect that it signifies to them a kind of judgmentalism or prudishness that seems unfashionable or even bigoted and repressive. I also suspect that there is much more to it than that; *sin* reminds us all of God, while our current use of *evil* finds a way to exclude him. We tend to use *evil* to refer to violations against our fellow humans, as the examples above indicate. *Sin*, however, is a word that has to do with our violations against God—attitudes, actions, and inactions that beset us all, but which we don't like to admit and which we masterfully cover up. *Sin* implies violations that are committed specifically against God, and this leaves our cultural gatekeepers unsettled. One way around this is to tone down the notion of sin; another way is to tone down the idea of God's holiness in favor of God's being "love." God's love is holy, and his holiness is loving—but for many these attributes seem to be mutually exclusive. Starting from that misguided notion, many people downplay anything that smacks of sin's being an offense against God; after all, "God is love," and love doesn't get bent out of shape over offenses.

Now, if a person's view of God/god is that he/she/it

doesn't really care about sin, that violations of God's will are no big deal, that "to err is human and to forgive is divine," then they will always diminish the magnitude of sin—and at the same time diminish the high price that sin extracts from us, the deep penalty that sin incurs. Minimizing sin in turn diminishes the eternal nature of God's justice, as well as the breadth of God's mercy. Great sin can be met only by great justice or a great salvation; sin that isn't so bad after all calls forth neither amazing grace nor fearful punishment. This shallow view of sin means that one can easily fall prey to giving cover for wickedness, excusing one's own fallen condition and actions, and, in the end, dismissing and/or diminishing the magnificence of Jesus and his loving sacrifice for us. The irony of arguing that, since God is love, sin isn't all that troublesome and forgiveness not all that costly, is that the love of God is made less important by this very attempt to exalt it. In order to exalt love, we must view sin clearly.

WHAT IS SIN?

Let's briefly tackle four dimensions of the biblical concept of sin, each of which deals with a different aspect of how our broken condition affects ourselves and others in relationship to God.

Sin is

- falling short of an established standard
- trespassing a forbidden border
- renouncing God's standards and inventing our own
- perverting the intent of our heart

In the first dimension, we "fall short of the glory of God" (Rom. 3:23). We were created as God's glorious image bearers; to perfectly obey his revealed will is our privilege and mission. Jesus meets this standard of love and holiness, but our own failure to do so is continuous and multifaceted. We love, but imperfectly and impurely; we pray, but half-heartedly and waywardly; we serve, but in hopes of being recognized and rewarded. Even if we know we are to be like Jesus, try as we may, we are not; when we think we are even coming close, we congratulate ourselves on the effort, defending ourselves against critics and boasting in our accomplishments.

In the second, something is forbidden to us, but we nevertheless take it; someplace is closed to us, but we sneak into it anyway. When I barge past the "No Entry Except to Authorized Personnel" sign, I am trespassing, and that word is exactly the one used by many of us when we pray the Lord's Prayer: "Forgive us our trespasses as we forgive those who trespass against us." Sin is trespassing a boundary that God has established for our good. For example, God's law forbids taking his name in vain, but in a whole host of ways, people are quick to use God's name as a curse but slow to offer him praise. We appear outwardly content, but inwardly we envy and covet our neighbor's portfolio and perfect career while craving the sexual satisfaction that we imagine his or her spouse would bring us. We say that we love, but the interior spaces of our souls scream hate.

The third dimension of sin is high treason against God, which is called *lawlessness* in the Bible. "Sin is lawlessness," wrote the apostle John (1 John 3:4). Lawlessness isn't simply failing to live up to God's law or standards, or trespassing the boundaries he has fixed for our good, but is instead the wholesale rejection of those standards and boundaries, together with God's right to establish them. Lawlessness says, "To hell with God and his standards! I am my own god; I am sovereign. *No one* tells me what I can or cannot do!" It's the path of radical personal independence that hates and despises God precisely because he has established standards and boundaries.

Even the lawless person soon discovers that he cannot live in total anarchy and so cunningly invents new standards and boundaries that he not only will live by but will usually demand that others submit to as well. Our culture may reject biblical norms of what constitutes blasphemous speech, but that doesn't mean that our culture doesn't have such laws, which are in many cases unwritten—for example, to say certain things in public or on social media is to risk job loss and worse.

The fourth way in which the Bible speaks of sin is the root of the other three. Our failure to meet standards, our entering the forbidden, and our tossing aside God's supposedly "repressive" and constricting laws all arise from a place deep within us that affects the totality of who were are. The Bible describes us as being enslaved to sin, bound up in iniquity, and "by nature children of wrath" (Eph. 2:3). *Sin* in this sense describes our very nature, from which arises all other faults, evil, and fallibility, plus all our failures to obey God—whether by what we have done or by what we have failed to do.

While sinful human beings—and that phrase describes us all—retain God's image,[6] at the heart of the human problem is the problem of the human heart: we are sinful people, and every aspect of who we are has been affected by this sad

6. Scripture refers to humans as beings that are unique among all God's creatures. Genesis records God saying of us, "Let Us make man in Our image, according to Our likeness" (Gen. 1:26), and this idea is carried throughout the Bible, serving as a warning to us against mistreating people, because all people are made in the image and likeness of God (see Gen. 9:6 and James 3:9–10). This "image" refers not to so much to our physical being as to our interior self—the realm of the soul. "For although God's glory shines forth in the outer man, yet there is no doubt that the proper seat of the image is in the soul" (John Calvin, *Institutes of the Christian Religion*, ed. John T. McNeill, trans. Ford Lewis Battles [Philadelphia:

and wicked situation. Some theologians describe this condition as *total depravity*. That doesn't mean we are as bad as we might be (we're not, and God's restraining hand in our lives and world keeps us from total annihilation), but rather that the totality of who we are as persons is infected with the virus of sin, which affects everything that we do. Sin runs deep. That's true even of our "good" acts. To put it simply, if I had a humble day, I'd be proud of it. Just as God's image is visible in the worst of sinners and abounds in the most grievous of sins, so too sin shows its ugly face even in my best efforts.

WHAT'S TO BE DONE?

Once we understand that we can't fix our need or extricate ourselves from our sin, we can finally begin to come to terms with God's solution to our predicament. The final nail in the coffin of our self-salvation projects comes when we acknowledge what the Bible teaches is the outcome and just penalty for our sin: death. We die because of sin, and we spread the infection and stench of death throughout all our institutions— political, economic, academic, and religious—even the ones that are created to be good. Envy, greed, abuse of power, and other maladies arise in our hearts, then go viral. We shouldn't be surprised by wickedness in high places when we realize that wickedness originates in the deep places of our own souls.

God's solution to our dilemma is summed up in the word *redemption*. Through redemption, God does not give us a "second chance" but instead gives us an entirely new life. He entered our world to save us by dying for us. He lived

---

The Westminster Press, 1960], 1.15.3). The Bible's referring to humankind as God's image bearers has to do with our spiritual, moral, volitional, intellectual, and communal selves.

the life we were called to live but can't and died the death we deserved to die but haven't. He doesn't ask us for our help; instead, through everything that he says and does, he shows that he alone can deliver us from the guilt and pollution of our sin. Christ's arrival on the scene is the ultimate sign that we cannot save ourselves—that Christ came to offer himself not first as an example for us to follow but as a Savior we can trust to deal with the totality of our brokenness: personally, culturally, and institutionally. In Christ alone, we find the deep forgiveness and freedom we need.

> Forgiveness does not come from doing good things, as if good deeds can erase what you have done. . . .
>
> The Bible you carry says it is better for a stone to be [tied] around your neck and you thrown into a lake than for you to make even one child stumble. And you have damaged hundreds.
>
> The Bible you [carry speaks of] a final judgment where all of God's wrath and eternal terror is poured out on men like you. Should you ever reach the point of truly facing what you have done, the guilt will be crushing. And that is what makes the gospel of Christ so sweet. Because it extends grace and hope and mercy where none should be found. And it will be there for you.[7]

So said Rachael Denhollander during the sentencing hearing of Dr. Larry Nassar. Nassar, a physician to female gymnasts, was convicted of systematically sexually assaulting hundreds of girls and young women, including Denhollander,

---

7. "Read Rachael Denhollander's Full Victim Impact Statement about Larry Nassar," CNN, January 30, 2018, https://www.cnn.com /2018/01/24/us/rachael-denhollander-full-statement/index.html.

and was aided and abetted by those who covered up his abusive behavior. One need not be a Christian in order to recognize that his actions were monstrous, to call for justice on behalf of his victims, and to work to make sure that such abuses don't recur. One must be a Christian, however, to give his actions the weight of eternity and to address him as Denhollander did.

Denhollander didn't gloss over Nassar's crimes and sins. Instead she pointed out the reality of temporal justice, which must be met, and of eternal justice, which would surely fall on him. She also pointed out the astonishing—and, to some, offensive—truth that mercy is real for those who repent. Just as sin flows from the sin-shattered heart, so too mercy can flow from the forgiven soul. She told Nassar that she would pray for him to "experience the soul crushing weight of guilt so [he] may someday experience true repentance and true forgiveness from God."[8]

If you were in deep poverty and you received a call from a credible friend and attorney that you'd just inherited a million dollars, you might be tempted to ignore the message or treat it like an email from a hacked friend asking you to send him money because he's stranded in Nigeria and can't get home. But you know the call is from a legit source, and, given your need, you can't afford to treat it with contempt. You have to at least check it out. What you'll discover if you begin to look into these claims about Jesus—what the Gospels say about his message and ministry, his life and death and resurrection from the dead—is that these reliable truths are transformational down to the core of the human heart, and from there out into every relationship and cultural activity. Scary thought? Absolutely. Because it's either true and we

8. CNN, "Rachael Denhollander's Full Victim Statement."

have to deal with it, or it's nonsense and we shouldn't mess with it for one more second.

The truth about Jesus is just what we need—though at first it appears more mysterious than reassuring. I know. We'll get to "reassuring." Here's the truth: our world is broken. I'm broken. You're broken. And we can't fix ourselves. Here's the good news: it's exactly at the point of the crack, at the place where we and our entire world are broken, that the light gets in. This Light has not come to expose and embarrass us like a reporter in search of the dirt; Immanuel, God with us, is not here to be some supernatural TMZ journalist showing up to highlight our mess. This Light comes to heal. This Light comes to rescue. This Light drives back the darkness— starting with the shadows that are lurking in our own souls.

"How?"

See you in the next chapter. It has a lot to do with the "cost" that Flannery O'Connor wrote about—the cost we would rather not consider in our misguided hope for quick fixes.

FOR REFLECTION OR GROUP DISCUSSION

1. In what ways do you see sin's brokenness in our society and in the church?
2. In what ways or circumstances have you had to confront your own personal brokenness?
3. "God is the great disturber." The author asserts that while God does bring peace, he brings about great discomfort in our lives as well. Discuss how these disturbances are God's acts of mercy and grace as much as his peace-giving is.
4. Discuss how a limited view of sin reduces rather than exalts our view of God's love.

5. Chapter 3 looks at four descriptions of sin. Look at Romans 3:23 and 1 John 3:4 and discuss how pervasive and deep sin runs in our lives.
6. How do Christ's life and death make redemption possible?
7. As a group, sing "Poor Sinners, Dejected by Fear" by William Gadsby.

4

CHRIST CRUCIFIED
The Indispensable Sacrifice

"How deep the Father's love for us."
—Hymn by Stuart Townend

*"He creates the universe, already foreseeing . . . the buzzing cloud
of flies about the cross . . . the nails driven through the mesial
nerves . . . the repeated torture of back and arms as it is time after
time, for breath's sake, hitched up. . . . Herein is love. This is the
diagram of Love Himself, the inventor of all loves."*
—C. S. Lewis, The Four Loves

Imagine starting a religious movement in the United
States with a lynching as its primary catalyst. Let's talk about
the reaction that would stir up and the possibility of success
that your new movement would enjoy. In the same way, if a
person living in the first-century Roman Empire wanted to
start a new religion that would attract as many adherents as
possible, he would never begin by centering this new religion

on a cross and a person who died on one. Yet within a few centuries of Jesus's death, the cross—this Roman sign of terror and shame—became a sign of God's love throughout the world.

If we understood how repugnant a cross was in the ancient world, we'd be astonished by this fact. In modern terms, lynching comes closest to crucifixion. Victims of lynching are often stripped, beaten, whipped, castrated, and hanged—in public for all to see—not only as "punishment" for a crime (which is, more often than not, a false accusation or a violated culture code) but even more significantly as a threat to others. Lynching keeps the oppressed in the gutter and the oppressors in power. Crucifixion was designed to torture victims for days before they finally died. The Romans used this form of punishment extensively, intending not merely to punish the enemies who suffered it with death, but to publicly humiliate them and turn their battered bodies into billboards for Roman power and justice. Both crucifixion and lynching are forms of public shaming, political point-making, torture, and execution—even murder.

The Romans viewed crucifixion in the worst possible light, though they nevertheless employed it on their enemies with great skill. The Roman rhetorician Cicero condemned it as "a most cruel and disgusting punishment."[1] He added, "To bind a Roman citizen is a crime, to flog him is an abomination, to kill him is almost an act of murder: to crucify him is—What? There is no fitting word that can possibly describe so horrible a deed."[2] And then, "The very word 'cross' should

---

1. Cicero, *Against Verres*, in *The Verrine Orations*, trans. L. H. G. Greenwood (London: Heinemann, 1935), 2.5.64, par. 165; quoted in John R. W. Stott, *The Cross of Christ*, 20th anniv. ed. (Downers Grove, IL: InterVarsity Press, 2006), 30.

2. Cicero, *Against Verres*, 2.5.66, par. 170; quoted in Stott, 30.

be far removed not only from the person of a Roman citizen, but from his thoughts, his eyes and his ears."[3]

The Jews shared this Roman disgust with the cross and were often themselves put to death in this terrible way by the Romans. For the Jews, no distinction was made between hanging someone on a cross or hanging someone on a tree. Being hung on a tree was a sign of being cursed by God, according to their own sacred text Deuteronomy 21:23. Trypho, an early Jewish opponent of the Christian faith, wrote in correspondence with a Christian apologist named Justin, "I am exceedingly incredulous" about a crucified Messiah.[4] Not only was the notion preposterous, it was heinous and offensive. It was, in Paul's words, "a stumbling block" and "folly" (1 Cor. 1:23 ESV).

Crucifixion was political. For the Romans, a crucified man hung on a cross because he had committed an act of treason or insurrection. Roman soldiers nailed Jesus to a cross because the Roman authority of his day viewed him as a dangerous criminal—a person capable of gathering an uprising to throw Jerusalem into confusion and Roman authorities to the dogs. From a historical standpoint, Jesus died on the cross for political reasons.

But something far deeper was going on.

THE CENTRALITY OF THE CROSS

The centrality of Jesus's death on the cross is found in every aspect of our Christian life together. When a child is

---

3. Cicero, *In Defense of Rabirius*, in *The Speeches of Cicero*, trans. H. G. Hodge (London: Heinemann, 1927), 5.16, p. 467; quoted in Stott, 30.

4. Justin Martyr, *Dialogue with Trypho a Jew*, in *The Ante-Nicene Fathers*, vol. 1, ed. A. Roberts and J. Donaldson (Grand Rapids: Eerdmans, 1981), chap. 89; quoted in Stott, 30.

baptized, in some traditions the sign of the cross is made on his or her head; Christian sermons declare that God's love is shown to us in the cross of Jesus Christ; Christians celebrate the Lord's Supper in worship, sharing in a ritual meal of bread and wine in obedience to Jesus's words to his disciples, "Do this in remembrance of Me," as he noted that the broken bread communicated his broken body and the wine his blood poured out on the cross (1 Cor. 11:24); we adorn our buildings with crosses, inside and out; ancient Christian sites and graves are marked by crosses; and many Christians wear crosses as jewelry or even tattoos. The cross is a pervasive presence in our faith.

Christians "boast" exclusively in the cross of Jesus Christ, just as Paul wrote in his letter to the Galatians (Gal. 6:14). He also wrote that his message could be summarized as "Jesus Christ, and Him crucified" (1 Cor. 2:2). For Paul, the message of the cross was the central teaching of the Christian faith. If Jesus is the indispensable person of the Christian faith, his death on the cross is the indispensable fact of the Christian life. A great hymn starts with the cross and ends with the words "Love so amazing, so divine, demands my soul, my life, my all."[5] Christians see the cross as a place where the love of God was shown to us, creating in us a response of devotion to and love for God.

JESUS'S VIEW OF THE CROSS

When we consider the cross of Jesus Christ, we need to remember that Jesus predicted his own suffering—in fact, he understood it to be the central purpose of his mission and life. Jesus Christ was born to die.

---

5. Isaac Watts, "When I Survey the Wondrous Cross," 1707.

Well before Jesus's statements about his own impending death, another Hebrew prophet, John the Baptist, identified Jesus as "the Lamb of God who takes away the sin of the world" (John 1:29). By introducing Jesus to Israel in this way, John referenced both Israel's deliverance from Egypt at Passover and Israel's sacrificial system, which was designed to deal with the guilt of sin and separation from God.

In the book of Exodus, God commanded Moses to have every family sacrifice a lamb and daub its blood on the top and the sides of the entryway to their home, then eat the lamb together inside as a sacred meal (see Exod. 12:1–28). While some of the details have changed (no one now ritually sacrifices a lamb and places its blood at their doorway), Jewish people around the world still celebrate the Feast of Passover through a family meal, in a beautiful rite that has been practiced continuously for some three thousand years. The blood of the lamb signified the faith of the people who were gathered in the home and delivered them from the death that came on all the firstborn of Egypt. Israel's sacrificial system was also instituted under Moses. On the great Day of Atonement, Yom Kippur, the priest offered a sacrifice that ceremonially took away the guilt of Israel's sins and reconciled the people to God.

Jesus began his public ministry with this in mind. He was the sacrificial Lamb. He repeatedly told his disciples that the day would come when he would go to Jerusalem and be handed over to the authorities there to be put to death on a cross. He described his approaching death as a grain of wheat falling into the ground and breaking apart, only to produce a harvest of life that would be many times greater than the size of the original seed (see John 12:24). While Jesus's opponents put him to death for politically expedient reasons, it was not politics that led Jesus Christ to the cross. It was love.

Jesus identified himself as "the Son of Man [who] came not to be served but to serve, and to give his life as a ransom for many" (Matt. 20:28 ESV). When Jesus said those words, he was quoting from the prophet Isaiah, who had spoken of Israel's future Messiah as a servant who would suffer on behalf of God's people. Isaiah described him as "a man of sorrows and acquainted with grief . . . one from whom men hide their faces" (Isa. 53:3 ESV). He added, "All we like sheep have gone astray . . . and the LORD has laid on him the iniquity of us all" (v. 6 ESV), and "with his wounds we are healed" (v. 5 ESV). By using the language of Isaiah 53, Jesus identified himself as that servant. His suffering would rescue his people who had gone astray, and he would take on himself their reproach and guilt.

We are fallen people, and our fall carries with it not only the terrible consequences of our sin but also real moral guilt before God, who created us. This is where Jesus's representative death on the cross comes into clear focus and why his blood shed for us is at the center of what it means to be a Christian.

OUR SUBSTITUTE

Can someone really die to take away the guilt of another person? People understandably feel that a sacrifice for sins is completely barbaric and objectionable. If the Romans objected to the message of the cross because crucifixion was repugnant, and if many Jews rejected the message of the cross because it claimed that someone who had been cursed by God was the Messiah, we moderns tend to reject the message of the cross because it offends our sense of how good we are while simultaneously diminishing the greatness and beauty of God's love. Basically, if God must be appeased by a blood sacrifice, some kind of "virgin in the volcano" human offering, then the message of Christianity is discredited; it is primitive superstition that is unworthy of sophisticated people and frankly horrifying. This is exactly what the message of the cross is not about.

We don't grasp the reality of Christ as the Lamb of God, our great substitute and sacrifice, because we fail to deal with three vital truths.

1. Our Guilt Is Grave

Human sin against God incurs guilt. We are legally accountable to God for our failure to do what he requires and for our ceaseless trespassing over the boundaries he has established. It isn't just that sin is destructive, though it certainly is; it's that we stand guilty before God because we have willfully gone against his perfect and holy will, justly deserve to be punished for our actions and inaction, and can do nothing to make up for the wrongs we have done. In addition, the penalty is more than we can bear—because God, the object of our sin, is eternal.

What can be done about this guilt? These are *our* sins; we must give some kind of account. If justice is to stand, then satisfaction for our guilt must be made.

We have an innate sense of justice and injustice. While every child has to be taught to say, "Please" and "Thank you," no child has to be taught to say, "That's not fair!" When we see injustice in our society, we recoil from it and want to see things put to rights. So it's no use saying that justice is unimportant to God. Our very human impulse has its root in the fact that we are made in God's image, and God himself is just—the very one who puts all things to right. God cannot let injustice stand.

Paul wrote, "None is righteous, no, not one" (Rom. 3:10

ESV)—every single one of us is a sinner before God, every single one of us must give an account to God for his or her sin, and every single one of us is guilty and is worthy of the punishment that is associated with our sinful treason against God. That penalty is death, considered in all its dimensions: physical, spiritual, relational, and eternal.

2. Our God Is Just

When people say, "God is love"—a statement that is certainly true—they sometimes mean by this that God does not have the capacity to hate. But love must hate some things, or it isn't love at all. If you love your children, you will hate a life-threatening illness that afflicts them; if you love your neighbor, you will hate to see him suffer. God hates—he hates sin.

God's antipathy to sin is seen in his wrath—his steadfast resistance to evil in all its forms and his perfect upholding of justice. Moreover, God, who is perfectly just, cannot deny himself. Were God to leave sin unpunished, were he to neglect people's just accountability for injustice and evil, then every being in the cosmos could accuse God of injustice. God is perfectly just in all his ways, and this means that the just requirement has to be fulfilled by him.

3. Our Substitute is Perfect

What God requires and commands in order to fulfill his justice, he lovingly and graciously fulfills in himself. God offers himself in the place of his sinful people, bearing himself their justly deserved punishment. What God commands for justice, he himself fulfills—because the penalty for sin is death, God himself died on behalf of those who deserved to die. In this way, God's astonishing love and unfathomable mercy are revealed in the cross of Christ, together with his justice. At the cross, God's holy love and perfect justice meet, for God the merciful forgives the sins of his wayward people by paying the price that his own justice rightly demands.

This is true because of the fact that God acts as our representative through Jesus Christ, who, as we have already noted, is both fully God and fully human. Jesus is the perfect and sole Mediator between God and humans because he is both God and human. He brings God to us, and he brings us to God. This is the idea of representation—something that we are largely unfamiliar with. We tend to view ourselves as standing alone and autonomous, acting on our own and for no one else with no one else representing us. The truth is that each of us impacts others through our actions. This is especially true when we have a particular role in some kind of social arrangement or relationship. When a president speaks, he represents an entire nation; likewise, parents' actions have consequences for their children, either for good or for ill. In the same way, Jesus Christ is our appointed representative, and his life and his death are accounted to us. In the same way that Adam's sinful actions brought death to the whole of humanity because he represented the entire human race, Jesus's perfect life and loving death brought life to all who claim him as their representative by trusting in him.

When Jesus Christ died on the cross as our representative and substitute—as the one on whom all our iniquities were laid—his blood became what Paul refers to as a *propitiation*. Now this is a word with which we are largely unfamiliar, and while we can't dig into it here as much as we should, we do need a basic understanding of this biblical term. In essence, a propitiation is something that turns away wrath—Jesus's blood satisfies the demands for holy justice because Jesus offers himself as the one who will absorb in himself all the penalties, all the justly deserved wrath, that his people deserved. He came to save his people from their sins, and he did so by his death.

In Romans 3, Paul says that this propitiation demonstrates God's justice—that God is both "just and the justifier of the one who has faith in Jesus" (Rom. 3:26). Paul notes that, far from requiring of people the full penalty of their sins, God had for centuries passed over them—he might well have been accused of being unjust, for he seemed to be delaying the sentence that should have been delivered. This delay came to an end at the cross, as Jesus bore in his own body our sins as he died, fulfilling all the claims of divine justice. Sin has been punished—and this is why God is seen to be just. God does punish sin; he does pour out his wrath—but he does this in such a way that, as the representative of his people, he bears that penalty himself. God the Son is the substitute for sinners so that they might be reconciled to God.

JUSTIFIED BY FAITH IN JESUS

Paul wrote that "God was in Christ reconciling the world to Himself" (2 Cor. 5:19), not counting our sins against us. This is why God is not only just but "the justifier of the one who has faith in Jesus." There are two sides to this idea of justification before God. On the one hand, our guilt before God is removed because Jesus's death has fulfilled the penalty of the law for our sins. But there is more. Justification is not only the removal of the guilt of our sins through Jesus's death but also the counting to us of Jesus's perfect life. Jesus's own perfect righteousness is given to us as a gift, freely and permanently.

Paul wrote that God "made Him who knew no sin to be sin on our behalf, so that we might become the righteousness of God in Him" (2 Cor. 5:21). In a moment of personal reflection, Paul said that he wanted to be found in Christ "not having a righteousness of my own that comes from the law, but that which comes through faith in Christ, the righteousness from God that depends on faith" (Phil. 3:9 ESV).

What Paul says in these two passages is extremely important. Paul notes, first of all, that on the cross Christ Jesus had counted to him our sin and in turn had counted to us his righteousness. This exchange is the incomparably good news of the gospel. Our sin was laid on Christ, and his righteousness was counted to us. Second, Paul says that there are only two ways of being righteous with God—the first being an attempt to keep God's law perfectly, for that is the requirement of the law. You can't pick and choose the commandments that you like, and "righteousness" means that you obey them all perfectly. The second is the polar opposite. Paul says the righteousness that he has in Christ is a declaration that God makes about him, a gift that was given to him from God, a righteousness that is not an achievement of our efforts but is a gift freely given that we receive by faith.

We have to deal with this choice between two paths of righteousness—one based on our performance and the other based on Christ's life and death. The choice could not be starker—for, as Paul has said, our only boast is the cross of Jesus Christ. In other words, these two potential paths are mutually exclusive. One cannot have righteousness through Christ and one's own performance as well. Jesus's work is perfect, and nothing can be added to it; indeed, the very notion of adding to what God has fully accomplished is not only absurd but offensive, for it is a denial of the sufficiency of what Jesus did on the cross. I can either have him as my Savior or try to save myself. The DIY approach to God negates grace and insults love; if it were possible for us to be right with God through our own works, then there was no need for Jesus to die. Yet Jesus did die on the cross after living a life of perfect obedience before the Father, who sent him to be our Savior.

Isaiah gets graphic about the idea that our own righteousness can save us; he reminded Israel that "all our righteous deeds are like a polluted garment" (Isa. 64:6 ESV)—a polite translation of a term that means used menstrual pads. That's us when we're doing our level best—not to mention how bad it is when we're at our worst. Paul was just as severe; referring to his own self-salvation efforts prior to his coming to faith in Jesus—all his religious pedigree, education, zeal, and attempts at obedience—he called them "dung," using a Greek word (*skubalon*) that we might translate less delicately.[6] Self-righteousness not only stinks; it's fatal. You can try to be righteous—right with God—on the basis of your work, or you can do what Paul did and says that we must do: rest in the perfect righteousness of Jesus that is freely given to us on the basis of what Jesus has done at the cross.

One Christian leader wrote of this remarkable gift,

The righteousness wherein we must be found, if we will be justified, is not our own . . . Christ hath merited righteousness for as many as are found in him. . . .

I must take heed what I say: but the Apostle saith, "God made him who knew no sin, to be sin for us, that we might be made the righteousness of God in him." Such we are in the sight of God the Father as is the very Son of God himself. Let it be counted folly, or [frenzy], or fury, or whatsoever. It is our wisdom and our comfort; we care for no knowledge in the world but this: *that man hath sinned and God hath suffered*; that God hath made himself

6. Let's just say that if chariots in Paul's day had been decorated with bumper stickers, one might have said, "Skubalon Happens."

the sin of men, and that men are made the righteousness of God.[7]

Martin Luther wrote to a friend, who was troubled by a guilty conscience, about this amazing gift of righteousness.

Oh, my dear brother, learn to know Christ and Him crucified. Learn to sing unto Him a new song, to despair of yourself, and to say to Him, "Thou, Lord Jesus Christ, art my righteousness, and I am Thy sin. Thou hast taken what was mine and hast given me what was Thine. What Thou wast not, Thou didst become, in order that I might become what I was not." Beware, my dear George, of pretending of such purity as no longer to confess yourself a sinner; for Christ dwells only with sinners. He came down from heaven, where He was living among the righteous, in order to live also among sinners. Meditate carefully upon this love of Christ, and you will taste all its unspeakable consolation. If our labors and afflictions could give peace to the conscience, why should Christ have died. You will not find peace save in Him, by despairing of yourself and of your works and in learning with what love He opens His arms to you, taking all your sins upon Himself and giving thee all His righteousness.[8]

The story of our life with Jesus in us begins with the story of Jesus's death for us. Because of the cross of Christ,

7. Richard Hooker, "A Learned Discourse on Justification," 1585; available online from Christian Classics Ethereal Library, https://www.ccel.org/ccel/hooker/just.html, emphasis added.

8. Quoted in Jean Henri Merle D'Aubigne, *The Triumph of Truth: A Life of Martin Luther*, ed. Mark Sidwell (repr., Greenville: BJU Press, 2007), 49–50.

our sins have been forgiven and we stand before God with the same perfect righteousness that Jesus himself possesses. No wonder all the company of heaven gather around the throne of grace and ceaselessly sing, "Worthy is the Lamb who was slain!" Jesus, the Lamb of God who died on the cross to take away our sins, has done absolutely everything required in order for us to be right with God. We aren't saved through anything that we do but by everything that he did for us. We dare not add to his work any of our own efforts, because these at their very best are all infected with our fallenness. Instead, we simply trust fully and completely in the perfection of his life and the propitiation of his death. He took our sin to the cross and the grave, and he gave his righteousness to us so that we could finally really begin to live and love.

When Jesus died on the cross, he cried out, "It is finished!"—and with those words announced that all the guilt of our sin had been taken away, permanently and completely. That means that the only thing still standing between God and us is our obstinate and foolish thought that we can save ourselves.

The benefits of Jesus's sacrifice become ours through one simple act: putting the whole weight of our lives, past, present, and future, into Jesus's cross-scarred hands. This act of trust is what the Bible calls faith, and it is faith that we will look at next.

FOR REFLECTION OR GROUP DISCUSSION

1. Both Cicero and Trypho are quoted in reference to the disdain with which the ancient Roman and Jewish societies viewed crucifixion. This means that shame was an especially poignant aspect of Jesus's suffering. How does his shame-bearing affect you?

2. Look at 1 Corinthians 1:18–23 and discuss the way in which the preaching of "Christ crucified" would have been heard by the people who were first listening to the apostles.

3. The author writes, "While Jesus's opponents put him to death for politically expedient reasons, it was not politics that led Jesus Christ to the cross. It was love." How was the crucifixion an act of self-giving love by Jesus, and what does it reveal to us about God? (See also Rom. 5:8.)

4. Read Romans 3:21–26. Discuss what impact the following words have on your understanding of the crucifixion of Jesus:
   a. *Redemption*
   b. *Propitiation*
   c. *Faith*

5. One of the central words in Romans is *justification*. The author notes two sides to this great truth. Look at 2 Corinthians 5:21 and discuss the dual imputation that is summed up in Paul's doctrine of justification.

6. The author writes, "When Jesus died on the cross, he cried out, 'It is finished!'—and with those words announced that all the guilt of our sin had been taken away, permanently and completely. That means that the only thing still standing between God and us is our obstinate and foolish thought that we can save ourselves." Discuss Jesus's words "It is finished" and how they impact your view of your relationship with God.

7. As a group, sing "O Sacred Head, Now Wounded," as translated by James W. Alexander.

5

FAITH

The Indispensable Gift

I gotta have faith.
—George Michael, "Faith"

But to the one who does not work, but believes in Him who
justifies the ungodly, his faith is credited as righteousness.
—Paul the Apostle

Just as the only basis for the removal of our guilt is the finished work of
Christ upon the cross in history, plus nothing, so the only instrument
for accepting that finished work of Christ upon the cross is faith.
—Francis Schaeffer, True Spirituality

"You won't believe this!" I love to hear those words. When my friends say this, I know I'm about to hear a story that's incredible—and probably pretty funny, too. I'm all ears.

About two thousand years ago, a "You're not gonna believe this" moment changed the world. Mary Magdalene, a follower of Jesus, visited his tomb before dawn on the third day after Jesus's crucifixion and found the grave empty. She ran back to Jesus's other followers to tell them that the body was missing. Not long after that, Jesus—raised from the dead—met Mary in the garden where he had been buried and told her to tell his disciples that he was alive. "You're not going to believe this," she said. Some didn't.

Jesus appeared to his disciples, and they saw his wounds—though absent Thomas famously and cynically dismissed the claims that Jesus was alive again because he hadn't seen him. Shortly thereafter, he ate his doubting words—his unbelief vanquished by Jesus's appearance to him a week later. "Put your finger here, and see my hands. . . . Do not disbelieve, but believe," Jesus said to him. "My Lord and my God!" Thomas confessed at the feet of the risen Savior. "Have you believed because you have seen me?" Jesus responded. "Blessed are those who have not seen and yet have believed" (John 20:27–29 ESV).

And there's the problem we face. I have never seen Jesus in person. I haven't placed my hand on his scars. Yet I believe in him. I believe that Jesus Christ is the risen Lord, my God, and the one through whom, by whom, and unto whom all things and persons exist. How is that possible? Why do I have faith, and what does it mean to believe?

Recently a friend of mine said to me, "I want to have faith; I want to believe. I just can't seem to do so. I don't know how that happens." He's not alone. Even those who saw Jesus in person had their doubts. After his resurrection, Jesus gathered his disciples together for his final commission to them and his ascension. "When they saw him they worshiped him, but some doubted" (Matt. 28:17 ESV). Worship and doubt hung out together on the mountain that day.

This is the case in the heart and mind of just about

every person I know, and certainly in every church that exists. We have faith, and sometimes it's actually pretty strong—but often it's weak. Some people find that the "faith thing" escapes them. Still others hate faith and ridicule belief. Celebrity atheist Richard Dawkins once quipped that not even Jesus's second coming would convince him that Jesus was the Son of God—he'd conclude that he was simply a being from a distant planet showing up on ours.[1] For Dawkins and other atheists who share his approach (though not all do), the universe is a closed system. There's no invisible world interacting with our visible world—predating it, shaping it, interrupting it, or erupting into it. Their anti-supernatural assumptions preclude the possibility of belief. For the rest of us—those who either are open to believing or have put our faith in Christ—the need of clarifying what faith is and what it means couldn't be more important.

BIBLICAL FAITH

If Richard Dawkins went to the doctor with a chest infection and was handed a prescription, he'd probably get it filled and take the medicine that the pharmacist (a "chemist,"

---

1. "I used to say [that what it would take for me to believe in God] would be very simple. It would be . . . the Second Coming of Jesus or a great, big, deep, booming, bass . . . voice saying, 'I am God.' . . . But I was persuaded, mostly by . . . Steve Zara . . . that even if there was this booming voice and the Second Coming and clouds of glory, the more probable explanation is that it's a hallucination or a conjuring trick by David Copperfield or something. . . . He made the point that a supernatural explanation for anything is incoherent. . . . It doesn't add up to an explanation for anything. A non-supernatural Second Coming could be aliens from outer space." Richard Dawkins, interview by Peter Boghossian (Portland State University, October 11, 2013), available online at https://www.youtube.com/watch?time_continue=2&v=qNcC866sm7s.

in Dawkins's England) handed him. My bet is that Professor Dawkins trusts his doctor and his pharmacist. He trusts their integrity and their skill; he trusts the manufacturers of the meds; he trusts the research that backs the prescribed treatment. And that's exactly what faith *isn't*.

Yes, faith—biblically considered—is trust in a person, but this biblical faith is trust in an unseen person who makes himself known to us through windows into ourselves, echoes of his activity in creation, occasional bright, blinding bolts out of the blue, and supremely in Jesus Christ revealed to us in the Scriptures. Dr. Dawkins's trip to the doctor and the pharmacist is an analogy of faith—a *ping* from the creation to the sonar of our souls. It shows how trust works. But authentic faith in Jesus Christ is first and foremost a gift that God gives rather than a product of our genius or experience.

"TRUST ME"

When I hear those words, my internal alarms go off. I start wondering what's for sale. "Take my word for it" is fine advice to act on if you know the person saying so; but if not, it's best to skip it—responding to the email asking you to deposit some cash in a church bank account somewhere in Africa is never a good idea.

When Jesus says, "Follow me" to his first disciples, they drop everything and go with him. But when they're stuck in a small boat in the middle of a raging storm at sea, they understandably panic. Jesus was asleep in the storm and perfectly calm. Not these guys; and I have to believe they had every reason to be worried—they were professional seamen who they knew what they were dealing with. They yelled at Jesus to wake up already and help them out. Jesus's response was to rebuke the wind and waves and calm the storm; he then rebuked their unbelief and unleashed a storm in their hearts. "Who is this guy? The wind and the sea obey him!" I'm guessing that the breakfast conversation among the disciples in the morning was, well, interesting.

The disciples were men of radical faith, who dropped everything in order to follow Jesus, and weak faith, who yielded in fear to their worst instincts to abandon Jesus. Yet that faith, which was sometimes weak and sometimes strong, was authentic. When Peter was on the cusp of denying, out of self-preserving terror, that he even knew Jesus, Jesus told him, "I have prayed for you that your faith may not fail. And when you have turned again, strengthen your brothers" (Luke 22:32 ESV). Peter was about to fail—famously and miserably and tragically. Jesus prayed for him. Peter failed, but his faith didn't. God-gifted faith—even when weak—is stronger than the sins we commit. That kind of faith doesn't originate in the fallen, fragile, fallible human heart. That kind of faith can come only from God.

What, then, is it?

FAITH IS A GIFT

In the Bible, *faith* is both a noun and a verb. Faith is something that we possess, and it is also something that we do. When we think about the noun, we typically use the word *faith* to refer to an attitude of the heart and the content of belief. When we think about faith as a verb, we typically use the word *believe* to express an action or a disposition of the soul toward God.

Faith is a gift that is bestowed by God on his people. Paul wrote to a group of Christians in the ancient city of Ephesus and reminded them that it was "by grace [that] you have been saved through faith" and that this faith was not from themselves but was "the gift of God" (Eph. 2:8). The faith by which we receive grace—even that is itself a grace. The power and presence of the Holy Spirit work faith in our hearts through the hearing of God's Word, and our faith is strengthened by our shared fellowship, worship, communion with God in the Lord's Supper, and prayer.

That's the first thing to know about biblical faith. The second is this: the gift of faith is the instrument by which we receive *all* the other gifts of God. The Bible repeatedly tells us that everything Christ has made available to us becomes our possession and inheritance by grace through faith. Faith isn't the basis on which God sends blessing into our lives, but it is the instrument by which he does so. The basis of our salvation is Christ's work on the cross—what he did!—not our faith, which is so unpredictable. Our faith is simply the way that the beauty of Jesus's gracious love becomes our own possession.

FAITH HAS CONTENT

When the Bible speaks of faith, it also has in view the content of our belief, which is sometimes referred to as "the faith." When Christians talk about our faith, we often mean the content of the doctrines that we hold to be true. For example, faith in Jesus means faith in a particular person who is revealed in Scripture, and, based on Scripture, the church holds to certain truths about who Jesus is and is not. This is also true of God the Father, God the Holy Spirit, the Scriptures, the church, and the requirements for all who profess to be followers of Jesus. The content of the faith is not something that individual believers craft on their own; rather, the content of our faith is rooted in the Scriptures themselves and has been articulated by the church in very careful terms over many centuries as summaries of belief.[2]

Faithful statements about the content of Christian belief ultimately direct us back to the Scriptures themselves. Jesus asked his contemporaries, "Have you not read what was said to you by God?" (Matt. 22:31 ESV). In saying this, he reminded them that, while the Scriptures are written in human languages and in particular historical and cultural settings, they are nevertheless God's own Word to his people for all time. The Holy Spirit directs us back to the Scriptures because, as Paul writes to the Romans, "faith comes from hearing, and hearing through the word of Christ" (Rom. 10:17 ESV). When we have faith in our hearts through the work of the Holy Spirit, we find ourselves embracing God's promises in the Scriptures, yielding our hearts to his commands, and seeking to have our minds renewed to his transforming truth.

FAITH BRINGS REST

How is faith most evident in our lives? The principal manifestation of faith in a heart that has received Christ is *rest*. As we saw in the last chapter, the finished work of Jesus Christ on the cross alone secures our deliverance from sin, death, and guilt, making us God's own children. This means that faith looks away from self and toward Christ, resting in Jesus and his finished work. I am safe in a relationship with God not because my faith is strong but because the object of my faith, Christ himself, is unshakable, unstoppable, unconquerable, and the Lord of all.

2. Important examples of these include the Apostles' Creed, the Nicene Creed, and the Athanasian Creed. Later statements like the Westminster Confession of Faith or the Augsburg Confession also contain doctrinal propositions that outline the content of the Christian faith.

British theologian John Barclay wrote, "The gospel presents the deeds of Christ in the first instance not so we can copy them, but so we can depend on them."[3] The essence of faith is rest in the life and death of Jesus—the author and finisher of my faith. My faith finds its origin in him, is being perfected in my life by him, and ultimately will take me to him.

This faith in Jesus Christ rests on the faith we have in the Scriptures, which testify to us about him. The scriptural witness arose in the ancient church, whose members willingly suffered painful, humiliating torture and death over what they knew to be factual. Their own blood sealed their testimony to the truth of the Scriptures' claims about Jesus Christ's being the risen Savior. The testimony of the church and her martyrs strengthens our faith also, pointing us to Jesus. We are, as the Scriptures say, "surrounded by so great a cloud of witnesses" (Heb. 12:1 ESV) who cheer us on as we wrestle with doubts and misgivings. These witnesses also faced doubts, but the gift of faith, which was created in them by the Holy Spirit, proved stronger than their doubts and carried them through great trials and pain.

Too often, young believers are discouraged from asking difficult questions about their faith and are told to "simply believe." In an interview with ESPN, Green Bay Packers quarterback Aaron Rodgers related such an experience. Rather than leading him deeper into the faith, it pointed him away from it.[4] Rodgers had been raised in an evangelical home and church, but the unwillingness of many Christians around

---

3. John M. G. Barclay, *Paul and the Gift* (2015; repr., Grand Rapids: Eerdmans, 2017), 110.

4. See Mina Kimes, "The Search for Aaron Rodgers," *ESPN the Magazine*, August 30, 2017, http://www.espn.com/espn/feature/story/_/page/enterpriseRodgers/green-bay-packers-qb-aaron-rodgers-unmasked-searching.

him to tackle the tough questions he was asking as he grew into a young man who was taking ownership of his own faith led him to view alternative spiritualities as more inviting and Christian faith as lacking foundation. We live in an age of cynicism and disbelief that are fueled by the suspicion that religious people are insecure and hypocritical in their faith. But tough questions have always been asked about the faith, and true faith does not squirm in their presence or shy away from looking for credible responses. Having faith in God does not downplay our capacity to reason and imagine, since that capacity finds its origin in God himself. The God who created your mind did not intend for you to ignore it or treat it with contempt.

The English poet Matthew Arnold noted that our modern era has seen the high tide of faith dissipate, which has left in its departure an age of confusion and despair.

> The sea of faith
> Was once, too, at the full, and round earth's shore
> Lay like the folds of a bright girdle furl'd;
> But now I only hear
> Its melancholy, long, withdrawing roar,
> Retreating to the breath
> Of the night-wind down the vast edges drear
> And naked shingles of the world.
>
> Ah, love, let us be true
> To one another! for the world, which seems
> To lie before us like a land of dreams,
> So various, so beautiful, so new,
> Hath really neither joy, nor love, nor light,
> Nor certitude, nor peace, nor help for pain;
> And we are here as on a darkling plain

Swept with confused alarms of struggle and flight,
Where ignorant armies clash by night.[5]

What a tragedy to live without joy, love, light, certitude, peace, or help in pain. How dark and foreboding! Yet that is all that the atheist can hope for: to seek enough pleasure or power to quiet the nagging sense that there is more to us than meets the eye, to salve the conscience that knows it cannot atone for its sins, to foster morality in a world that mocks everything but what technology can achieve.

Christian faith is not a philosophy. It is not a set of ideas that are suspended in midair and unrooted from the soil of our experience and our history. Our faith is in a person who lived and died and rose again from the dead. Our faith is rooted in historical events that are described in historical documents. It is rooted in our shared struggle to understand those events and what they mean about the person at the center of those events—namely, Jesus Christ. Faith seeks understanding and embraces the adventure of learning every day while joyfully resting in Jesus's perfect and saving work.

When we have faith, we will also wrestle with doubt; our faith feels sometimes very strong and at other times very weak. Like Peter, we sometimes have the faith to step out of the boat toward Jesus and walk on the water. Like Peter, we sometimes tremble at the raging waves and lose sight of our Lord. Yet in the midst of our doubts, in the midst of our weak faith, we find a faithful Savior. When Peter began to sink, Jesus reached toward him, took him by the hand, pulled him up, and walked with him over the waves and back to the boat. Our faith in Jesus comes from Jesus. The faithful Savior sustains us.

5. Matthew Arnold, "Dover Beach," in *New Poems* (London, 1867), 112.

You may have a weak faith that you wish were stronger, but you have a strong Savior who could not be more powerful. If you are his, it is not because your trust never wavers but because his love never fails.

FOR REFLECTION OR GROUP DISCUSSION

1. Faith is sometimes seen as irrational. Is this true of faith in Jesus Christ as the Savior of sinners? If not, why?

2. Sometimes people suggest that faith means the absence of doubt. Give some examples of when Jesus's own disciples had both faith and doubt at the same time and how they learned to grow in faith.

3. Paul wrote that faith was a gift that God bestows. Look at Ephesians 2:8–10 and discuss God's mercy and the gift of faith.

4. Sometimes people are described as being a "person of faith"—as though trust in some kind of spirituality, something religious, or some kind of god or gods is in itself commendable. Does this use of the word *faith* fit Christianity, or does the content of what is believed actually matter? If so, why; and where in Scripture would you point someone to look who disagreed with this, in hopes that their understanding might be enlarged?

5. Why is rest such a key dimension of what it means to have faith in Christ?

6. Discuss this statement and then make it the basis of prayer together. "You may have a weak faith that you wish were stronger, but you have a strong Savior who could not be more powerful. If you are his, it is not because your trust never wavers but because his love never fails."

7. As a group, sing "Jesus, Lover of My Soul" by Charles Wesley.

6

ETERNAL LIFE

The Indispensable Hope

And I saw a new heaven and a new earth.
—John the Apostle

Time . . . takes everybody out. It's undefeated.
—Rocky Balboa, Creed

The words "Wait until next year" are precious to every sports fan—they sum up the resigned despair that fans feel after a favorite team finishes the season with less than a championship (and sometimes with gut-wrenching losses) as well as the indomitable hope they feel that the championship will be won in the season that's on the distant horizon. "Sure as God made green apples," said legendary baseball broadcaster Harry Caray, "someday, the Chicago Cubs are gonna be in the World Series."[1] Harry didn't live to see it happen, but the Chicago

---

1. Caray delivered this quote while covering the Cubs' final game of

Cubs did, in fact, not only *reach* the World Series but—finally, after 108 seasons of "Wait until next year"—*win* it. When the team pulled off the long-hoped-for accomplishment, some fans went to Harry's grave in the Chicago suburbs, draped it with Cubs pennants and hats, and deposited around it several baskets of little green apples. It was a touching tribute. Harry's predicted "someday" had come.

I was at the game in Cleveland when the Cubs won the Series, simultaneously shouting and weeping for joy as the final out was made. I still cry when I think about it. I'd been waiting for that moment for half of those 108 years; I had buried some fellow fans who "died in hope" and had watched boyhood heroes like Hall-of-Fame Cubs players Ernie Banks and Ron Santo exit this life without ever seeing their team reach the summit of the baseball world. Waiting is tough—and it's worse when you know, going into some seasons, that your team really doesn't have a chance at all.

While some fans thought that the Cubs must be cursed, the truth had a lot more to do with down-to-earth organization and players than with metaphysical mysteries. The team just hadn't yet put together a championship organization and team. When that changed a few years ago, the championship followed—and I hope many more will follow in the coming years. After that 2016 World Series championship-clinching game against the Cleveland Indians, the baseball season ended without my saying, "Wait until next year"—for the first time in my life. "Next year" had finally become "this year." All my long-cherished hopes had finally been realized.

"Let me tell you something, my friend. Hope is a dangerous thing," says Red in *The Shawshank Redemption*, my

---

the season, against the St. Louis Cardinals on October 6, 1991, reporting from Wrigley Field in Chicago for Chicago's WGN-TV.

second-favorite movie (and favorite Stephen King novel). "Hope can drive a man insane."[2] The movie is set in a prison—a place where hope goes to die a slow and miserable death; though one prisoner, Andy Dufresne, keeps hope alive and finally escapes into the freedom that should always have been his. That doesn't diminish the truth of Red's claim. Hope, in the sense that he uses the term, is exactly what can be the undoing of our interior lives: "Hope deferred makes the heart sick" (Prov. 13:12).

BIBLICAL HOPE

The kind of hope we have been looking at so far—the hope of fans for a championship or of a prisoner for liberty—may be compelling and even beautiful in some ways, but it isn't at all what the Bible has in view when it speaks of hope. Biblical hope is very different indeed. A fan may hope his team will win in the future, but he doesn't *know* that they will. A prisoner may hope for freedom, but he doesn't *know* that he will be liberated. These future hopes are painful precisely because they represent a lack of assurance about the future. "All we have is hope"—because certainty is impossible.

Biblical hope, by way of contrast, is all about the certainty now of what is yet to come. Yes, biblical hope is about the future; but that's where its similarities with regular hope end. Our hope is eternal; hope and faith and love form the triplet virtues of the Christian life. Our hope is not about *whether* Christ will come again, or *whether* we will be raised with him, or *whether* the heavens and earth will be made new in the perfect kingdom of Jesus Christ. Our hope is simply about the timing

2. "The Danger of Hope," *The Shawshank Redemption*, directed by Frank Darabont (1994; Burbank, CA: Warner Home Video, 1999), DVD.

and shape of these sure and certain realities. Christian hope is not about *whether* Christ will come again but about *when* Christ will come again. Right now we don't see all that we want to see; and so, Paul writes, we are saved in hope (see Rom. 8:22–24).

I feel the tension between what we long for and what we experience right now—as well as exactly how biblical hope meets it—every time I stand at the graveside of a believer. Palpable sadness envelopes the mourners like a dark cloud. In the middle of the pain of the sting of death and the finality of the grave, it's my calling to commit the body of the deceased to the earth—"ashes to ashes, dust to dust"—and the soul to the God of all mercy and grace, all "in the sure and certain hope of the resurrection."[3] What an astonishing phrase— *sure and certain hope.* That would be an oxymoron were it not for the biblical view of hope that is rooted in Jesus Christ's resurrection. That event—the bodily resurrection of Jesus from the dead three days after his crucifixion—meant that the future, the long-hoped-for resurrection of the dead, had been dragged kicking and screaming into the present. Resurrection from the dead is real—and the living Christ proves it. From that moment, everything in the world changed; and the power of death itself was broken forever.

> In hope we have been saved, but hope that is seen is not hope; for who hopes for what he already sees? But if we hope for what we do not see, with perseverance we wait eagerly for it. (Rom. 8:24–25)

> Now faith is the substance of things hoped for. (Heb. 11:1 KJV)

3. "The Order for the Burial of the Dead," from the Book of Common Prayer (1662).

We are "saved in hope"—but what is it that we hope to see? What future realities give shape to our present lives? Let's look at three great hopes we have that are rooted in Jesus's resurrection, which the Bible boldly sets forth as transforming the way that we view everything we experience now.

1. THE RETURN OF CHRIST

In his letter to Titus, Paul refers to Jesus Christ's return as the "blessed hope" of believers.

> The grace of God has appeared, bringing salvation to all men, instructing us to deny ungodliness and worldly desires and to live sensibly, righteously and godly in the present age, looking for the blessed hope and the appearing of the glory of our great God and Savior, Christ Jesus. (Titus 2:11–13)

Don't miss how Paul ties our expectation of Christ's return in the future to the way we are called to live right now. The apostle teaches us that what has happened in the *past* (the grace of God that has appeared, bringing salvation) and what will happen in the *future* (the second appearing of Christ Jesus) reshapes how we live in the *present*. Between what God has done and what he will yet do, he summons us to live an entirely new kind of life that is characterized by wisdom and holiness. What we believe about the past and the future is our front door to living as faithful Christians right now.

Christians hold different views on exactly how the future appearing of Christ will unfold—some even offering misguided, and always wildly inaccurate, predictions about the date it will occur. Such silliness is something of a cottage industry in the United States, where people are often swept up by end-of-the-world prophecies. Perhaps the most famous of these was "The Great Disappointment"—the aftermath of William Miller's prediction that the second coming would take place in March 1843. His followers—upward of a hundred thousand people—sold their homes, quit their businesses, left their families, and gathered together to await Christ's return . . . which, of course, did not occur.[4] Because Jesus said, about the entire matter, "That day and hour no one knows" (Matt. 24:36), we can safely set aside unprofitable speculation in favor of something more orthodox and helpful.

Whatever our differences, we confess together in the Apostles' Creed that we "believe in one Lord Jesus Christ . . . who will *come again* to judge the living and the dead, whose kingdom will have no end." The return of Christ is predicted first and foremost by Jesus himself. As the Savior ascended into glory, angels also announced his return, promising Jesus's disciples who were staring heavenward in awestruck wonder that "this Jesus . . . will come in just the same way as you have watched Him go" (Acts 1:11).

The apostles wrote about Jesus's expected and longed-for return in several places, and at the core of these promises we discover hope. This biblical hope is our comfort and strength, especially in the face of death's great onslaught.

> We do not want you to be uninformed, brethren, about those who are asleep, so that you will not grieve as do the rest who have no hope. For if we believe that Jesus died and rose again, even so God will bring with Him those

---

4. The secular version of this fascination is a constant theme in "the end of the world as we know it" movies. From *The Day after Tomorrow* and *2012* to post-apocalyptic sci-fi like *I Am Legend*, *Planet of the Apes*, and just about every zombie franchise you can think of, Hollywood has its own way of tapping into our dread and hope about the climax of history.

who have fallen asleep in Jesus. . . . For the Lord Himself will descend from heaven with a shout . . . and the dead in Christ will rise first. Then we who are alive and remain will be caught up together with them in the clouds to meet the Lord in the air, and so we shall always be with the Lord. Therefore comfort one another with these words. (1 Thess. 4:13–14, 16–18)

For as in Adam all die, so also in Christ all will be made alive. But each in his own order: Christ the first fruits, after that those who are Christ's at His coming, then comes the end, when He hands over the kingdom to the God and Father, when He has abolished all rule and all authority and power. . . . The last enemy that will be abolished is death. (1 Cor. 15:22–24, 26)

For many people, the idea of God writing "The End" is a terrifying prospect; and in our culture, visions of the Apocalypse are almost always tales of violence, horror, disintegration, and fear. On closer examination, it's clear that what many hold to be signs of the end are nothing of the kind; they are simply characteristics of the labor pains of an age that is yet to break in on the world. Jesus said that everything would proceed as normal until the day it was—quite suddenly!—too late.

Of that day and hour no one knows . . . but the Father alone. For the coming of the Son of Man will be just like the days of Noah. For as in those days before the flood they were eating and drinking, marrying and giving in marriage, until the day that Noah entered the ark, and they did not understand until the flood came and took them all away; so will the coming of the Son of Man be. Then there will be two men in the field; one will be taken and one will be left. Two women will be grinding at the mill; one will be taken and one will be left. (Matt. 24:36–41)

One of the more insidious and sadly popular views of Jesus's second coming is the so-called "rapture" of the church off the earth. I got caught up in "rapture fever" in the mid-1970s when I was in my teens. I'd read a popular and convincing book on the second coming of Christ, and, doing the math, we could be pretty certain that the world wouldn't last much past 1988 or so. The second coming would happen in stages: first, the secret removal (rapture) of true believers from the earth; second, the horrors of the seven-year "great tribulation," when the earth would be ruled by the antichrist; finally, the return of Jesus, who would come back with all the raptured, whack the Antichrist, and retrieve anyone left on earth who had bravely refused the "mark of the beast" (the dreaded 666) and were counted as faithful. (In all likelihood, this would be a small group, since most everyone who didn't bow to the powers during the great tribulation would have already suffered a brutal martyr's death.) Confused? I don't blame you.

A bunch of us started getting ready for the rapture; just in case the theory was a little off and we had to ride it out all the way to the end, we got ready for the great tribulation too. Together with a good friend who was old enough to drive, we headed to an Indiana field to bury some Bibles in case ours were confiscated by the forces of the Antichrist during the coming days of darkness. Spurred on by a baptized survivalist impulse, we drove through the gate into a pasture, buried our box of Bibles with fervent prayer, and then noticed a herd of cattle heading for our little Honda Civic. We raced back to the car and got in, but we were completely surrounded and unable to move in any direction. We prayed. Nothing. . . . The cows closed in. A curious wet nose pressed against my window. We "rebuked" the cows, commanding them to move "in Jesus's name!" Nothing. Desperate, we tried what anyone with a brain would have suggested: hit the horn. At its blast, the cows hustled away, and we escaped our own personal apocalypse. I got home thinking that my views on Jesus's second coming needed some recalibrating.

Jesus said, "One is taken and one is left." But who's taken and who's left? In the escapist vision of the future, the good guys "fly away" and the bad guys are "left behind" to endure the trauma of the coming evil days. In fact, a closer look at Matthew 24 shows that the "taken" refer to those who, as in the days of Noah, were "taken away" in judgment. Those "left" were Noah and his believing family, safe in the ark—the meek inherited the earth. So we await the Savior's return; but he is coming not to take us away but to bring about the final glorification of creation and of his people. We're glad to be the ones left behind, who will inherit the earth "at the end of the age. The Son of Man will send his angels, and they will gather out of his kingdom all . . . law-breakers. . . . Then the righteous will shine like the sun in the kingdom of their Father" (Matt. 13:40–41, 43 ESV). Confessing that Christ will "come again with glory to judge the living and the dead" shapes how we live now—with vibrant expectation, watchful diligence, faithful service, and unyielding love in a cold, dark age that will one day yield to the fullness of the one who is the Light of the World.

2. THE RESURRECTION OF THE DEAD

Even if we don't like to discuss it or deal with it—I can tell you that not many people actually preplan their funeral arrangements—we are all going to die. The artists in our society stand as prophets who point out the obvious and get us back to reality through their stories. It's why Eliot must be heeded and *Hamilton* is correct when it says that death is an insatiable, equal-opportunity thief that takes life without reference to whether a person believes or doesn't.[5] We can dress up death and avoid the subject; we can bury people in places that are far removed from our worship; but we can't permanently drive away the shadow of death.

The ancient world's experience of death was more dreadful than our own. Life expectancy in the Roman Empire of Paul's day was around twenty-one—a figure that was depressed by massive infant mortality and by the death of mothers in childbirth. Disease was rampant, violence endemic, and human life cheap. People could and did live long lives, but they were the exceptions. People tended to believe in existence after death but faced death with fear and loathing; their vision of the afterlife, which was solidly in the grip of Platonism, left people disembodied and consigned to the shadows.

Into this scene burst the Christian message of hope: Christ had been raised from the dead—bodily!—and death was thus overcome. This message was met with ridicule by some in the elite, educated spheres of Roman society: "When they heard of the resurrection of the dead, some began to sneer" (Acts 17:32). Others, however, wanted to know more. This was, after all, radically hopeful news. If Christ had been raised from the dead, then everything had changed. People believed in *existence* after death, but *resurrection* from the dead was something altogether different.

5. See Leslie Odom Jr., vocalist, "Wait for It," by Lin-Manuel Miranda, recorded August 2015, track 13 on act one of *Hamilton: Original Broadway Cast Recording*, Atlantic, 2015.

Paul preached Christ crucified and raised from the dead—Christ dying for our sins and being "raised for our justification" (Rom. 4:25 ESV). The writer of Hebrews tells us that God entered the world as one of us "that through death He might render powerless him who had the power of death, that is, the devil, and might free those who through fear of death were subject to slavery all their lives" (Heb. 2:14–15). Jesus's resurrection was central to the Christian message. "I delivered to you as of first importance what I also received, that Christ died for our sins according to the Scriptures, and that He was buried, and that He was raised on the third day according to the Scriptures" (1 Cor. 15:3–4). And no wonder! The implications of Jesus's bodily resurrection are massive and absolutely central to our view of biblical hope.

Mourners have taught me more by their grieving faith than I have ever taught them in a homily or eulogy at a funeral service. One moment stands out in my experience. An elderly woman, a beautiful member of the church I served, had been married to her husband for over sixty years. At her funeral, her husband shook my hand, thanked me for my message, and turned to the open casket in order to pay his final respects. He gently placed his hand on it and bent over, kissing his beloved's forehead one last time, and said words I will never forget: "I will see you in the morning." I knew he had kissed her and said those words ten thousand times in his life. Now he said them in the face of death. That's biblical hope for the resurrection. We face death saying, "I will see you in the morning." How is this possible?

Paul noted several factors about Jesus's resurrection that we have to take to heart (see 1 Cor. 15:12–19). When some of the Corinthian Christians lost sight of this indispensable truth, Paul noted the sad implications of denying the bodily resurrection. His logic is relentless. If the resurrection of the dead is a myth, then Christ has not been raised—Jesus is dead. If Jesus is dead, then our preaching is false and our faith is worthless. If Jesus is dead, the entire "Christian faith" is a pitiable lie, and the sins we have committed still weigh us down to judgement. Not only that, but all the Christians who have died are lost forever. Jesus is just one more good teacher we can listen to in an effort to make this life a bit better; we can hope in Christ for this life but not the next; he's a possible "life coach," but a Savior from death and hell is exactly what he isn't.

Then Paul turns the table and outlines the powerful hope that we have as believers in Jesus who was raised from the dead—the conqueror of the grave and sin. Just as we surely died "in Adam," we are destined for resurrection because we are now "in Christ." The resurrection of the dead that we will inherit through Jesus is as sure and certain as the death we've experienced because of the fall.

> But Christ has indeed been raised from the dead, the first-fruits of those who have fallen asleep. For since death came through a man, the resurrection of the dead comes also through a man. For as in Adam all die, so in Christ all will be made alive. (1 Cor. 15:20–22 NIV)

What will that look like? Paul outlines it as total transformation, in which we don't lose who we are but become fully and truly what we've always been created to be in Christ. Loosed from the grip of sin and death, and restored to the full beauty of immortality, we enter the new age of eternal communion with God and perfected community with one another, free from tears and fears. He alludes to Isaiah, who portrayed the end as a great feast at which God "eats" death, "swallowing" it up and giving us the feast of his beauty and grace in place of death consuming us. Isaiah wrote, "On this mountain the LORD Almighty will prepare a feast of rich food for all peoples, a banquet of aged wine—the best of meats and the finest of wines. . . . He will swallow up death forever. The Sovereign LORD will wipe away the tears from all faces" (Isa. 25:6–8 NIV). God is the ultimate "death eater," who, by ingesting this dread foe, secures our feast of beauty and hope.

Here's how Paul relates that promise from Isaiah in terms of Jesus's resurrection, as he makes clear that death is not our final destiny. We will be "changed" not by death but by resurrection. The victory of Jesus over death is now our victory as well. We still feel the sting of death, but at the resurrection, when our sure and certain hope is fully and finally realized, that pain will be no more. We don't deny the pain or the grief of death; on the contrary, we embrace it *in hope*.

> Behold, I tell you a mystery; we will not all sleep, but we will all be changed, in a moment, in the twinkling of an eye, at the last trumpet; for the trumpet will sound, and the dead will be raised imperishable, and we will be changed. . . . "Death is swallowed up in victory. O death, where is your victory? O death, where is your sting?" The sting of death is sin, and the power of sin is the law; but thanks be to God, who gives us the victory through our Lord Jesus Christ. (1 Cor. 15:51–52, 54–57)

Paul calls this ultimate victory that will be graced to us in Jesus "the redemption of our body" (Rom. 8:23), and he goes on to describe the event as the moment when the current "body of our humble state" will be transformed "into conformity with the body of His glory" (Phil. 3:21). In other words, the resurrection of Jesus is the prototype of our own—we have died with him, and we shall be raised with him. "As we have borne the image of the earthy, we shall also bear the image of the heavenly" (1 Cor. 15:49 KJV). What a hope!

In the Eastern Orthodox funeral tradition, the priest says a prayer on behalf of the deceased. It's a beautiful commentary on our hope: "Of old Thou hast created me from nothing and honored me with Thy divine image. But when I disobeyed Thy commandment, thou hast returned me to the earth whence I was taken. Lead me back again to Thy likeness, refashioning my former beauty."[6] Death is not the end; Jesus, who is the "Resurrection and the Life," the one who by death trampled down death, will raise us to share in his immortal life—in the beauty that was lost and then restored by redemption. This is exactly the hope that is at the root of an epitaph that Benjamin Franklin wrote for his gravestone. While it wasn't ultimately used, it's a beautiful summary of how we view death and decay in the hope of bodily resurrection.

> The Body of
> B. Franklin,
> Printer;
> Like the Cover of an old Book,
> Its Contents torn out,
> And stript of its Lettering and Gilding,
> Lies here, Food for Worms.
> But the Work shall not be wholly lost:
> For it will, as he believ'd, appear once more,
> In a new & more perfect Edition,

6. *The Lenten Triodion*, tr. Mother Mary and Archimandrite Kallistos Ware (London: Faber, 1978), 128; quoted in Bishop Kallistos Ware, *The Inner Kingdom*, The Collected Works 1 (Crestwood, NY: St. Vladimir's Seminary Press, 2000), 31.

Corrected and amended
By the Author.[7]

The results of our hope are manifold in this life. We no longer fear death as the final note in the symphony of our lives. We grieve and feel the sting of death, but even our grief is shaped by hope—our tears never run down our faces absent the comforting grace of God. We "encourage one another" (1 Thess. 4:18 ESV) with the hope of the resurrection and our reunion with those who have gone before us—those who have already "fallen asleep" in Jesus (v. 14). Have we buried our parents? Our children? Our friends? Our spouses? They are not lost; with them we enjoy the "communion of the saints" and "wait for" resurrection morning. We will see them in the morning.

We also know that what we do with our lives has eternal significance. Our lives are a "breath" that quickly passes, and we could be tempted to feel that we and our work have no lasting value. The resurrection negates that lie. Life may be short, but what we do in it now counts forever. Paul concludes his discussion of the resurrection in the future with good counsel for how we should live right now: "Therefore, my beloved brethren, be steadfast, immovable, always abounding in the work of the Lord, knowing that your toil is not in vain in the Lord" (1 Cor. 15:58).

A memorial marker in St. Giles Street, Oxford, has a wise and well-known proverb on it:

Remember me as you pass by
As you are now so once was I

7. Available online at "Epitaph, 1728," National Archives, accessed October 12, 2018, https://founders.archives.gov/documents/Franklin/01-01-02-0033.

> As I am now so you shall be
> Prepare for death, you follow me

One morning I noticed that someone had written some rather clever graffiti under it, adding to its potency.

> To follow you I'm not content
> Until I know which way you went!

While the vandalism was quickly rectified, the truth of its message remains. When Jesus comes again, and the dead are raised, some will be raised to eternal life in his presence—others to eternal darkness away from the beauty of his glory. Trusting Christ the Death Defeater in this life opens the door to eternal life for us all.

3. THE RESTORATION OF CREATION

When Christ returns, he will return to the created world, and our resurrection from the dead will be the glorification of a part of creation: our own bodies and souls. That's why we can't imagine for a second that biblical hope is divorced from creation, from the visible world around us, which writhes in pain because of our sin and also bears faithful witness to God's majesty through its beauty. God will not abandon his creation but will instead "make all things new." This "newness" is not a replacement of this created cosmos but rather its renewal and renovation—its own resurrection. In Ephesians, Paul describes the restoration of all things as the end that God has always intended for Jesus's saving mission: "He made known to us the mystery of His will . . . that is, the summing up of all things in Christ, things in the heavens and things on the earth" (Eph. 1:9–10).

In the fullness of time, God will reunite heaven and earth in a restored harmony of grace that will free the creation from its current slavery to the fall. Paul speaks of this in Romans, connecting it with our own personal resurrection from the dead.

> The anxious longing of the creation waits eagerly for the revealing of the sons of God. For the creation was subjected to futility, not willingly, but because of Him who subjected it, in hope that the creation itself also will be set free from its slavery to corruption into the freedom of the glory of the children of God. For we know that the whole creation groans and suffers the pains of childbirth together until now. And not only this, but also we ourselves, having the first fruits of the Spirit, even we ourselves groan within ourselves, waiting eagerly for our adoption as sons, the redemption of our body. (Rom. 8:19–23)

We are still dealing with the aftermath of our fall—with the prospect of death and with our ongoing fight with sin in all its forms. In this moving passage, Paul tells us that the "groanings" we experience now are shared by creation. Our struggle, which will ultimately give way to our glory, is paralleled by creation's—and both struggles will have the same outcome: freedom. Our saving hope is not confined to our human bodies but extends to all creation, for Jesus has come to save the world. The entire created order, which currently strains under the weight of our tragic rebellion, will enjoy the fruit of our redemption. In J. R. R. Tolkien's magnificent *Return of the King*, Sam, one of the Hobbit heroes, encounters Gandalf after he has been raised from the dead, and exclaims, "Gandalf! I thought you were dead! But then I thought I was dead myself. Is everything sad going to come untrue? What's happened to the world?"[8] The answer that Christian hope offers to Sam's question is resounding: "Yes, the sad is coming untrue" and "Behold, I saw a new heavens and a new earth . . ."

My mom is in Christ's presence, and I look forward to seeing her again in the resurrection. That future hope ripens with every passing year, swallowing up the pain and sorrow of what was, for me, her untimely death. When I was a small boy, she would gather us around an old upright grand piano and we would sing hymns. Her favorite—and one that we sang a lot!—was "This is My Father's World," and it gave me a robust theology of creation's coming redemption. I close this chapter with those words that were taught to me by my mother—who, with my dad, instilled in me the sure and certain hope of the resurrection. My friend, the battle is not done; but Jesus who died will be satisfied and earth and heaven be one.

> This is my Father's world:
> Oh, let me ne'er forget
> That though the wrong seems oft so strong,
> God is the ruler yet.
> This is my Father's world,
> The battle is not done:
> Jesus who died shall be satisfied,
> And earth and Heav'n be one.[9]

---

8. J. R. R. Tolkien, *The Return of the King* (1955; repr., New York: Mariner, 2012), 903.

9. Maltbie D. Babcock, "This is My Father's World," 1901.

FOR REFLECTION OR GROUP DISCUSSION

1. What is the difference between the way we commonly use the word *hope* ("I hope our team wins"; "I hope that investment succeeds") and biblical hope ("In hope we have been saved")?

2. How does our hope for the future return of Christ shape the way that we live right now?

3. What are some of the problems with a wrong-headed preoccupation with the second coming, or with believing that its date can be predicted?

4. Carefully read Matthew 24:36–44. The wicked were "taken away" in the flood. What are the implications of this in verses 40–41? Who is taken? Who is left?

5. Talk about this statement: "The implications of Jesus's bodily resurrection are massive and absolutely central to our view of biblical hope." Why is this so?

6. Is "resurrection" the same thing as the continuing existence of the soul after death, or does it mean more than this?

7. How is creation affected by sin, and how will it be changed by the resurrection of the dead and the return of Christ? How does this affect your own view of creation?

8. Jesus has promised a "new heavens and new earth." Discuss what this means and how his promise shapes our lives today.

9. As a group, sing "Lo! He Comes with Clouds Descending" by Charles Wesley.

7

LOVE

The Indispensable Virtue

Love one another, even as I have loved you. . . . By this all men will
know that you are My disciples, if you have love for one another.
—*Jesus Christ*

My weight is my love.
—*St. Augustine,* Confessions

The chief goal of most instruction is a transfer of information, but that is exactly what the goal of Christian disciple-
ship is not. "The goal of our instruction," wrote Paul, "is love
from a pure heart and a good conscience and a sincere faith"
(1 Tim. 1:5). In other words, the sum of Christian disciple-
ship is not theological precision, or the ability to recite vast
amounts of Scripture, or even the dutiful embrace of various
spiritual disciplines; it is instead the formation of a life that
is characterized by God's love flowing from a heart that has
been made pure by mercy.

An authentic Christian life is marked by the indispensable virtue called love. It is by our love for one another, Jesus taught, that people will know we are his disciples (see John 13:34–35). That's an astonishing statement. People know Jesus's followers not by the power of their miracles, the devotedness of their prayers, the eloquence of their sermons, the wisdom of their sages, or the beauty of their art, but rather by a single, unmistakable quality: their love. I wonder if we truly believe this.

If the Christian community neglects the poor, embraces injustice, supports powers that tyrannize the weak, neglects orphans and other children, and treats fellow humans as anything less than God's image-bearers, people have every right to question the validity of our claims. If we refuse to forgive one another, segregate the church over race and politics, and won't work to heal the many divisions in the body of Christ, should we really be shocked that our cold indifference to the unity for which Jesus prayed leaves the world convinced that we have little to offer them in terms of hope and kindness? It may be that some of us are leaving the kind of unpleasant impression that was captured so well by John Steinbeck in his description of the "tight, hard . . . humorless as a chicken" wife of Samuel Hamilton: "She had a dour Presbyterian mind and a code of morals that pinned down and beat the brains out of nearly everything that was pleasant to do."[1]

THE GREATEST OF THESE

One of the most beloved passages of Scripture is 1 Corinthians 13, in which Paul praises the beauty of love. "Love," Paul writes,

1. John Steinbeck, *East of Eden* (1952; repr., New York: Penguin Books, 2002), 9.

is patient, love is kind and is not jealous; love does not brag and is not arrogant, does not act unbecomingly; it does not seek its own, is not provoked, does not take into account a wrong suffered, does not rejoice in unrighteousness, but rejoices with the truth; bears all things, believes all things, hopes all things, endures all things. Love never fails. (1 Cor. 13:4–8)

That these words are held in such high regard is ironic, because those who first heard them were being rebuked and corrected. The Corinthian church to whom Paul addressed his letter was perhaps the single most disjointed and problematic congregation that anyone can imagine. Filled with pride over various gifts of the Spirit and badly divided over everything from economic status and preferred preachers to ethnicity, they got drunk at communion, neglected basic standards of holiness, and squabbled over who among them was more spiritual rather than actually tackling the tough issues.

Paul mercifully lowers the boom on this terrible situation by bringing to the Corinthian Christians' attention the one virtue that would correct every problem.

If I speak with the tongues of men and of angels, but do not have love, I have become a noisy gong or a clanging cymbal. If I have the gift of prophecy, and know all mysteries and all knowledge; and if I have all faith, so as to remove mountains, but do not have love, I am nothing. And if I give all my possessions to feed the poor, and if I surrender my body to be burned, but do not have love, it profits me nothing. (1 Cor. 13:1–3)

Why was the church so badly disordered? They had forgotten Christianity's most basic truth: we are the beloved of God, and so we love one another. The Corinthians might have been known for their "spirituality," but that was an empty boast. Their lack of love showed, and that lack undermined everything that they claimed for themselves.

The beautiful treasures of faith that I am describing in this book would be for nothing if they were not formed in our souls by God's love and manifested in our lives by the same. Love is the single greatest virtue, as Paul noted: "Now abide faith, hope, love, these three; but the greatest of these is love" (1 Cor. 13:13 NKJV). According to John, love is the hallmark of the true Christian: "We know that we have passed from death to life, because we love each other. Anyone who does not love remains in death" (1 John 3:14 NIV). Christian love, as Christopher Wright points out, "is a matter of life and death. It's as serious as that. It's what proves you have passed from one to the other."[2]

Love is the authenticating mark of the believer, and its lack the warning light that a faith professed is not a faith possessed. John writes,

> Beloved, let us love one another, for love is from God; and everyone who loves is born of God and knows God. The one who does not love does not know God, for God is love. . . . We love, because He first loved us. If someone says, "I love God," and hates his brother, he is a liar; for the one who does not love his brother whom he has seen, cannot love God whom he has not seen. (1 John 4:7–8, 19–20).

If we actually expect others to be open to the gospel that we share with them, then we must also embrace the reality that

---

2. Christopher J. H. Wright, *Cultivating the Fruit of the Spirit: Growing in Christlikeness* (Downers Grove, IL: InterVarsity Press, 2017), 26.

it is not first our words but our lives—and especially the lives that we live as a community of sacrificial, serving, forgiving believers—that make Jesus and his gospel beautiful and believable. Francis Schaeffer summed this up well when he wrote, "The church is to be a loving church in a dying culture. . . . In the midst of the word . . . Jesus is giving a right to the world. Upon His authority He gives the world the right to judge whether you and I are born-again Christians on the basis of our observable love toward all Christians."[3]

Love lives at the heart of our faith because it is the single virtue that summarizes the very being of God. God *is* Love. When we believe and receive God's love for us, hear Jesus's command to love one another as he loved us, recognize that the command to love God with our whole being is the single greatest commandment, equaled only by the second—to love our neighbors as we love ourselves—and know that the credibility of our confession is at stake, then we take this subject seriously indeed.

THE LOOK OF LOVE

English is a beautiful and flexible language, but it does have its drawbacks—one of which is our limited vocabulary for *love*. In the course of a single day, I might easily say, "I love the Texas Longhorns," "I love my wife," "I love coffee," "I love cooking," "I love reading," "I love great music," "I love my dog," and "I love Jesus." Does the word *love* carry the same meaning and weight in each phrase? Do I have the same kind of affection for and devotion to my favorite college football

3. Francis A. Schaeffer, *The Mark of the Christian*, in *The Complete Works of Francis A. Schaeffer: A Christian Worldview*, vol. 4, *A Christian View of the Church*, 2nd ed. (Wheaton, IL: Crossway, 1985), 187.

team as I do for Jesus?[4] Typically, we listen between the lines. When someone says that they love the movies, we know they're not using the word *love* in the same way that they did when they told their future spouse, "I love you" for the first time.

Thankfully, that ambiguity does not exist in the New Testament. The New Testament was written in Greek, and, unlike English, the Greek language deploys four distinct words for love: one for erotic sexual desire, one for friendship, one for affection, and one, *agape*, for sacrificial self-giving for others. While scholars note a degree of overlap among these words, the distinction between them, especially when it comes to describing profound and deep love, is easily seen.[5] The Bible recognizes that all four loves are God-created and God-given (even if we twist them into something that barely resembles their original intent), but it is the final one—*agape*—that Jesus employs when he commands us to love as he loves; it is the same word that Paul uses when he writes that love never fails and the word that John pens when he asserts, "God is love."

Agape means "self-giving"—indeed, giving of self to the point of deep suffering and sacrifice. It is the love of a parent who dies to save her child. It is the love of a neighbor who bears the cost of another's recovery, even if it means painful loss. It is the cross-shaped love of God that bears every insult and sin in order to win back the souls of beings who made the cross and spikes that killed the Savior in the first place. It is this

4. To be fair, I do know some people for whom that might be true— but that indicates a problem to be dealt with rather than a quality to be encouraged!

5. C. S. Lewis wrote a very helpful book, *The Four Loves*, on these different words, which goes deep into the way that these different words show up in classical culture and how this impacts our view of love when it comes to our faith.

sacrificial, self-giving aspect of *agape* that John summarized so powerfully when he wrote, "This is how we know what love is: Jesus Christ laid down his life for us. And we ought to lay down our lives for our brothers" (1 John 3:16 NIV). The King James Version of the Bible translates this word as "charity" in 1 Corinthians 13 to make a clear distinction between this gift-love and all other loves. Without this love, there is no such thing as Christian faith in my heart, for if I "have not charity, I am nothing" (1 Cor. 13:2 KJV).

We may well go on using the word *love* in a popular or merely erotic sense, and there would be nothing wrong with doing so. The problem arises when we use different senses of the word as equals. If by *love* I mean "erotic passion" and then conclude that eroticism is at the top of the virtue pyramid because "God is love," I am not only abusing the language but participating in a revolution designed to overthrow the real meaning of love. Erotic desire can be good or bad; it can flourish as joy in the beauty of marriage or decay into death at the core of unbridled, violent outbursts of self-satisfaction that is pursued at the expense of others. Gift-love—*agape*, the Love that is God and that God gives in Jesus through the Holy Spirit—is the exact opposite. It spends itself for the sake of the other, seeking not its own satisfaction but the safety and good of the beloved. Other loves may take or bargain, but this love bleeds and gives. Erotic love may rightly confess, "I cannot live without her"; but agape love says, "I will die for you, my dearest, that you might live and know joy."

RISKY LOVE

Love in this sense truly is reckless. Relentless and unstoppable, it takes no thought for itself but runs toward the object of its sacrificial desire in order to bring life and hope. It is the love of the first responder who moves into the flames to rescue another or of the soldier who hurls himself onto a live grenade to save his brothers-in-arms. It is Dr. Martin Luther King Jr.—who, knowing that his life was under constant threat, boldly stepped into the hatred of others in order to secure peace. He chose to overcome a long history of racist violence, not by returning evil for evil but by offering a different path. "Darkness cannot drive out darkness; only light can do that. Hate cannot drive out hate; only love can do that," he wrote.[6]

At the core of this love is a sense of being compelled to act. "My weight is my love," wrote Augustine, using *weight* in the ancient sense of gravitational pull—love that roots our lives in beauty.[7] What we love both grounds us and moves us inexorably toward the object of that love; it transforms us. Because God is love, he does not grow in love; but, being Love, he cannot remain in isolation from the suffering of his people whom he cherishes. He must move toward them with rescuing love that takes the shape of a sacrifice. His very being is sacrificial.

This is why it's so wrong-headed to imagine the cross as some kind of payment to satisfy God's offended honor or to quiet his petulant temper. At the cross, Paul writes, "God shows his love for us" (Rom. 5:8 ESV). The cross is the ultimate demonstration of *agape*—of self-giving—for in it, God, who is love, moves toward his broken and bound people to heal and rescue them, not by offering them a repair manual or a medical prescription but by entering their pain and giving himself over to death. God is the first responder to the human

6. Martin Luther King Jr., *Strength to Love* (New York: Harper & Row, 1963; repr., Minneapolis: Fortress Press, 2010), 47.

7. "Pondus meum amor meus." St. Augustine, *Confessions*, 13.9.

condition, running into the flames of our disaster to rescue us from the fire we started.

This reminds us that God's love pursues those who reject and hate him. God loves his enemies and, through that love, brings them to life. This is why the love to which we are called as Christians is also so very different from that which passes for love in the common culture. Summoning his disciples to follow in the path of redeeming love, Jesus said,

> You have heard that it was said, "Love your neighbor and hate your enemy." But I tell you, love your enemies and pray for those who persecute you, that you may be children of your Father in heaven. . . . If you love those who love you, what reward will you get? Are not even the tax collectors doing that? And if you greet only your own people, what are you doing more than others? Do not even pagans do that? Be perfect, therefore, as your heavenly Father is perfect. (Matt. 5:43–48 NIV)

What does love look like? It looks like God the helpless babe lying in a food trough at the margins of the world, among the poor. It looks like a famished man battling hell in a desert. It looks like befriending the people everyone else rejects. It looks like liberating the people no one can tolerate. It looks like healing the people who have no hope. It looks like a Master washing the feet of servants who would deny and betray him. It looks like dying for the people who want to kill you. Love looks like Jesus. Jesus is the Word made flesh—the love language of God.

When we hear this language and learn to speak it as well, we position ourselves as a prophetic people in the world who demonstrate, by word and deed, the cross of Christ. This is the position that we see in Dr. King's 1957 Christmas Day sermon as he called us to demonstrate sacrificial love in the face of anger. He wrote, "Hate multiplies hate, violence multiplies violence, and toughness multiplies toughness in a descending spiral of destruction. So when Jesus says 'Love your enemies,' he is setting forth a profound and ultimately inescapable admonition. Have we not come to such an impasse in the modern world that we must love our enemies—or else? The chain reaction of evil—hate begetting hate, wars producing more wars—must be broken, or we shall be plunged into the dark abyss of annihilation."[8]

WALK IN LOVE

My friend Gerrit spent a morning with Mother Teresa in Calcutta. As they discussed worship, Gerritt hoped to impress on her the need for her and her sisters to sing beautiful songs of praise and thanks to God. Mother Teresa answered that singing did not play a large role in her worship. "What does worship mean to you, then?" Gerritt asked. "If you really want to worship," she answered, "go out and serve the poor and sick; care for those in need; for, as Jesus taught us, 'In as much as you've done it unto the least of these, you've done it unto Me.'"

I love this very true story, because it rebukes our tendency to identify our love for God and others with what we might think of as "religious" activity. Paul the apostle taught that our whole lives are to be lived in love. "Walk in love, as Christ loved us and gave himself up for us," he wrote to the ancient Christians (Eph. 5:2 ESV). Paul would have us learn that "all of life is love for God."[9]

8. See King, *Strength to Love*, 47.

9. John W. Sanderson, *The Fruit of the Spirit* (repr., Phillipsburg, NJ:

This command from the apostle follows his exposition in Ephesians 2:1–10 of God's gracious initiative to save us through the unmerited mercy and grace of Jesus. Paul introduces the ethics of how we are to live after rooting us in the grace that has brought us to life, wording his command to love, itself, in such a way that we see our call to love as an expression of the love that Jesus has bestowed on us. John takes the same approach when he writes, "We love because he first loved us" (1 John 4:19 ESV). This love from God, which is "poured into our hearts through the Holy Spirit" (Rom. 5:5 ESV), not only brings us from death to life but teaches us the way to live every day. No area of life is untouched by Jesus's reign of grace, and therefore no area of our lives is not transformed by love.[10] From friendship to family and from work to worship, our lives are to be shaped by love, thereby pointing others to the one who is Love.

Not everyone says yes to the love of God, and many will also say no to the same love as it is shown in our lives. Pain and suffering will accompany our lives of risky love. But the only alternative to the pain of love is to withdraw our hearts from engaging with others. The outcome of that course is not only fatal but damning:

> To love at all is to be vulnerable. Love anything, and your heart will certainly be wrung and possibly be broken. If you want to make sure of keeping it intact, you must give your heart to no one, not even to an animal. Wrap it carefully round with hobbies and little luxuries; avoid all

---

P&R Publishing, 1985), 49.

10. This is reflected in the title and subtitle of my colleague and friend Scotty Smith's beautiful book *The Reign of Grace: The Delights and Demands of God's Love* (West Monroe, LA: Howard Publishing, 2003).

entanglements; lock it up safe in the casket or coffin of your selfishness. But in that casket—safe, dark, motionless, airless—it will change. It will not be broken; it will become unbreakable, impenetrable, irredeemable. The alternative to tragedy, or at least to the risk of tragedy, is damnation. The only place outside Heaven where you can be perfectly safe from all the dangers and perturbations of love is Hell.[11]

LOVE IN ACTION

"The fruit of the Spirit is love," Paul wrote (Gal. 5:22)—but what does that fruit taste like? Love is tangible and can't be reduced to an internal emotion that may or may not result in action. Agape love is especially concrete and is embodied in movements of costly care and compassion. That's exactly the point of Jesus's story of the unexpected love of the Samaritan in Luke's gospel.

When a master theologian tried to test Jesus about the greatest commandment of all, Jesus asked him what he read in the law. The man answered, "You shall love the Lord your God with all your heart and with all your soul and with all your strength and with all your mind, and your neighbor as yourself" (Luke 10:27). Jesus responded, "You have answered correctly; do this, and you will live" (v. 28). Then things got dicey. The man wanted to extend the conversation and narrow down the definition of *neighbor* to make sure he was "doing it right." Luke continues, "But he, desiring to justify himself, said to Jesus, 'And who is my neighbor?'" (v. 29).

Jesus answered the man in the form of one of his most well-known parables—that of the Good Samaritan. In Jesus's

11. C. S. Lewis, *The Four Loves* (New York: Harcourt, Brace & World, 1960), 169.

story, a Jewish man traveling alone on the Jericho Road is beaten and left to die on the side of the road. Other travelers, including a priest and a Levite, pass by and see him in pain but offer no aid to the victim of the attack; all of them hurry on, unwilling to take the risky step of stopping to help. The twist in the tale is next. A stranger approaches on the road; seeing the dying man, he is moved by compassion and stops to tend to his wounds. The stranger picks him up and carries him to an inn where he can receive more care and can fully recover, telling the innkeeper, "Here's the money for his care, and I'll pay the price of whatever else is needed to restore him to health." The astonishing thing is that the stranger who stops to help the Jewish victim of violence is a Samaritan man—the last kind of person who anyone listening to Jesus would have expected to show mercy. Jews and Samaritans despised one another. In this Samaritan, however, love and mercy were more powerful than hatred and division. "My neighbor" is not only the person near me who is like me and whom I find easy to love; my neighbor is anyone who is in need of mercy, regardless of any ethnicity, ancient hatreds, or past sins. "Neighbor love" is defined as mercy for all, rather than as help for some when it's convenient for me.[12]

In Jesus's story, we can identify with the injured man on the side of the road, with the religious leaders who preserved their purity and schedules by ignoring him, and maybe even with the robbers who inflicted the injured man's suffering. Jesus is the ultimate outsider who comes on the scene to rescue us, doing for us what religion cannot and will not do—charging the cost of our recovery to his own account. The point of his mercy and love, however, cannot and must not be left at that important gospel note. The love that brings us

---

12. See Luke 10:30–37 for the full parable.

back to life is the same love that we are called to show with our lives. We are called to identify with Jesus and his love for a neighbor—with the unexpected sacrifice for someone who is *different* from us . . . someone, indeed, who is our sworn enemy.

I suspect that the men who passed by the injured, broken man on the road to Jericho had very good reasons for doing so—things they were sure God had put on their day planners and that thus required their undivided attention. In fact, like them, we need to recognize the everyday, unscheduled opportunities we have to be vessels of the rich mercy we have received. Love cannot ignore the broken in the name of punctuality or purity.

Yet there is more to this than the overthrow of inconvenience and mere religion. It is the shocking love of the outsider for the insider, of the hated for the hater, of the victim for the perpetrator.

We can understand the relish every jilted lover feels when they discover that their "ex" is now in pain. We can all understand the satisfaction that victims of a war have in the conquest and punishment of the people who caused their suffering. Those feelings arise from forms of love as well—from self-love and love of country. But what of the warrior who loves and forgives his foe? What of the rejected groom who welcomes back the runaway bride who broke his heart? It is this latter, more difficult-to-grasp kind of love that the cross shows us. It calls us outside the boundaries of our personal chronologies, national prejudices, and long-held pain into the upper reaches of a deeper love that finds its origin in God. By this love we see people differently; we see them more in keeping with how God sees them, and this transforms the way that we treat them.

THE WEIGHT OF GLORY

St. Mary's Church in Broad Street, Oxford, has witnessed some of the most famous sermons in history, including Thomas Cranmer's final sermon before he was hurried away to be burned at the stake. In more recent times, no sermon has resonated more deeply than "The Weight of Glory," which was given in the church by C. S. Lewis. In his message Lewis noted that there is a burden-bearing quality to our relationship with one another that is eternal in nature and is shaped every day by the way we treat each other in very temporal matters of life. He famously observed, "There are no ordinary people. You have never talked to a mere mortal." The point, he went on to make clear, is that every person we meet—people we may be tempted to ignore or even despise—are immortal souls who are headed toward an eternal destination that will reveal them as being either a nightmarish "horror" or a creature that we might deem worthy of worship because of its fantastic splendor. This means that our interactions with all people must be marked by what Lewis calls "real and costly love," for *in* our Christian neighbors Christ is truly hidden, and *to* our non-Christian neighbors Christ remains hidden while we yearn for them to see his glory.[13]

This is why love for one's enemies stands as a crystal-clear beacon in the teaching of Jesus. His contemporaries were all well-versed in the ethic of returning evil for evil in the name of justice. Christ reverses this with his commandment to love as he has loved—to love one's enemy to life. This is exactly what he did at the cross, forgiving those who sought his death and who hung him there to perish in pain.

13. See C. S. Lewis, *The Weight of Glory: And Other Addresses* (San Francisco: HarperOne, 2001), 45–46

Love my enemies? I don't even like them. Herein lies the most visible section of the vast chasm between my Creator-Redeemer-Sustainer and me. When I hated him, he loved me. I am nothing like this Savior-God—no, not one bit. It must be that grace alone remains the antidote for my fall and my self-preservation. And only by that same grace can I love as he loves—for the glory of the Father and the love of his Beloved and his enemies.

Loving our enemies does not mean that we understand them or find their company desirable. That is to confuse *agape* with other, lesser loves. Speaking of Jesus's command to love our enemies, Dr. King wrote, "We should be happy that he did not say, 'Like your enemies.' It is almost impossible to like some people."[14] No—the cross-shaped love of God in Christ, which is poured into our hearts through the Holy Spirit, offers the deep gifts of forgiveness, mercy, and kindness without reference to compatibility or mere affection. This love seeks the good even of those who offer only hate in return and whose company, at least in our current state, would be undesirable.

Let's make this real. Who thinks that *you* are the enemy? Who do you think is "the enemy"? What are you doing today to show the person who thinks you're part of the problem that you are actually part of the solution? What are you doing today to delegitimize the hate and rage that rocks and divides our daily discourse? Are you "leading with love"—or with your politics and pet causes that allow you to define the boundaries of who you will care for? If your de-churched, never-churched, LGBTQ, agnostic, atheist, Hindu, Muslim, Buddhist, Mormon, or even Baptist neighbor thinks the thing that most characterizes you is your opinion rather than your love, you're doing it wrong.

14. King, *Strength to Love*, 46.

WHERE IS LOVE?

In March of 1995, a ninety-three-year-old man died in a small town in Poland. His name was Franciszek Gajowniczek. The death of an elderly man might not strike us as significant, but his long life was due to the death of another man in his place. At the outbreak of WWII in 1939, Gajownicek, then a soldier in the Polish army, had been captured by advancing Nazi troops. He was sent to Auschwitz, where he was prisoner 5659. That's when prisoner 16670 steps into the story.

While at least 1.5 million Jews perished in Auschwitz and its neighboring camp Birkenau, evidence indicates that hundreds of thousands of non-Jews were also murdered. Among these were Polish intellectuals who were feared by the ascendant Nazi regime, including the Catholic Franciscan leader Fr. Maximilian Kolbe. This man—prisoner 16670—was standing with the other prisoners in roll call when the camp commander demanded that ten men be starved to death as punishment for the disappearance of three prisoners from the camp. One of those selected for death was Gajownicek. When chosen, he cried out for mercy, speaking of his wife and children and pleading to be spared. Hearing his cries, Fr. Kolbe stepped forward and offered to take Gajownicek's place among the condemned; his offer was accepted.

Very little can prepare a person for the horror of Auschwitz. I've walked around the nightmarish camp—the ground zero of evil in modern history. I've been in the dark corridors of the basement cell block and stared into the cell where Kolbe wasted away without food and water before finally being put to death by lethal injection. Kolbe's willingness to sacrifice his life for another prisoner made him, in Pope John Paul II's words, a "martyr of charity."

"The opposite of love is not hate, but indifference,"

said Elie Wiesel, describing the horrors of Auschwitz.[15] His masterful memoir *Night* points out that the great danger, the great opposite of love, is a life of detachment. That cannot be an option for us. At the intersection of division, rage, and self-seeking pride, the witness to Christ's self-giving love has the most impact. We must choose love, God's love, and make it the quality that people think of first when we come to their minds.

One does not need to be a Roman Catholic in order to recognize, in Fr. Kolbe's sacrifice of self for another, an embodiment of the loving death of Jesus on our behalf and an example of what it means to love our neighbor. Gajownicek spent the rest of his life telling others of the man who died so he could live. We do this as well; but we do it most effectively when we tell it in deeds of mercy that match our words of grace.

We live in a world in turmoil—a world that's in need of people who will forgive extravagantly, love unexpectedly, and serve joyfully. It is not simply that in the course of our day we encounter Jesus in our neighbors who do believe, as Lewis makes plain in *Weight of Glory*; but that we are able to offer Jesus to our neighbors who do not yet believe. In nearly forty years of ministry, I have yet to meet a single convert who was brought to Christ through the anger of a Christian. Never. Millions, however, may be won by love.

It is God's lovingkindness that has made us his own. It is God's lovingkindness, shown in his people, that will bear witness to the cross and show others the path of life. It is the love of God, given to us and shown through us in acts of engaged

---

15. Elie Wiesel, interview by Oprah Winfrey, *O, The Oprah Magazine*, November 2000, available online at http://www.oprah.com/omagazine /oprah-interviews-elie-wiesel/2.

kindness, that gives others a glimpse of his compassion. It is his love ablaze within his people that supplies the strength we will need to bear the weight of our neighbor's glory. Let those who have been loved first love themselves less for the sake of those who have not known this love at all.

FOR REFLECTION OR GROUP DISCUSSION

1. Why does Paul make "love from a pure heart" the goal of his apostolic teaching? How does this differ from the ways in which we tend to think of instruction more generally—or even to think of it in the Christian church?

2. Read 1 Corinthians 13. Discuss in what ways this chapter is a rebuke meant to correct rather than a "sweet" passage meant to bring comfort.

3. The author writes, "Love is the authenticating mark of the believer, and its lack the warning light that a faith professed is not a faith possessed." Look at several different passages of Scripture in this chapter that affirm this assertion, and discuss why love must be the mark of the Christian.

4. People need to be loved in ways that express love in terms they understand. Discuss how the church sometimes fails to say, "I love you" to the unbeliever just when the church thinks it's being loving.

5. Augustine wrote, "My weight is my love." What did he mean by this? How does this relate to God's love for us? In what ways do you see this principle at work in your own life?

6. Neighbor love, as expressed by the Good Samaritan, is love in action. Talk about this parable in connection to C. S. Lewis's observation on carrying the weight of our neighbor's glory.

7. Discuss Lewis's words "There are no ordinary people. You have never talked to a mere mortal." How does this shift your perception of your daily routine?

8. As a group, sing "Love Divine, All Loves Excelling" by Charles Wesley.

8

JUSTIFICATION
AND ADOPTION
The Indispensable Relationship

All forgiveness, then, is costly.
—*Tim Keller,* Counterfeit Gods

It is not imitation that makes sons.
It is sonship that make us imitators.
—*Martin Luther,* Lectures on Galatians

I'm not an especially good traveler—especially on long flights. One of the wilder experiences I've ever had was a flight from New York to Tel Aviv, on which numerous children were very active and very loud. As I tried to get some rest, I was annoyed by one little boy in particular who kept running up and down the aisle, yelling at the top of his lungs, "Abba! Abba!" I remember thinking that his parents ought to get him under control, that his sheer delight in seeking out their attention was driving everyone else a little crazy. Of course, as soon as that thought passed through my mind, a very different thought settled in as well. I remembered that Paul used the very same word when he described the way our hearts cry out to God the Father through Jesus Christ his son. Paul wrote, "God has sent the Spirit of his Son into our hearts, crying, 'Abba! Father!'" (Gal. 4:6 ESV).

Abba is an ancient Aramaic word that is used of an intimate, personal, affectionate relationship between a child and his father. We might use the word *Papa*. It's the word that Jesus used in prayer when he spoke to God, and it's the word that Jesus gives to us in our prayers. The astonishing truth is that we are now also God's children, and we speak to God the Father with the very same word that Jesus used. We call him Papa.

BELOVED CHILDREN

Lin Manuel Miranda's incredible musical *Hamilton* is a sensation, drawing thousands and thousands to its compelling performances. The show opens with an introduction to the title character through the eyes of his contemporaries. His arch-foe, Aaron Burr, starts by emphasizing Alexander Hamilton's lowly origins: he was an illegitimate orphan surrounded by sin, poverty, and squalor. How did he rise to become a Founding Father of the United States?

Hamilton's dire beginnings are an apt summary of our own. We are originally the sons of Adam and the daughters of Eve. The ill effects of their treason against God yielded its bitter fruit in us, too, so that we were God's enemies, opposing him and his ways at every step. We are "by nature children of wrath" (Eph. 2:3), and it's astonishing that any of us rise from the ash heap of human ruin to the throne room of

God's glory. How can sinful people have a relationship with God that is deeply personal and affectionate? How can that possibly happen?

In short, it's a gift. When God bestowed his love on us through Jesus Christ, our representative, something amazing happened. When Jesus died on the cross, he bore our guilt and shame—all those things that were impediments to our relationship with God—and took them with him to his death. Paul puts it this way: "[God] made him to be sin who knew no sin" (2 Cor. 5:21 ESV).

As we've seen in previous chapters, that's just the first part of an incredible exchange that God's grace engineered. As our royal representative, Jesus Christ took on himself the full responsibility and guilt of the wrongdoing of all those who are his people. When he died, he cried out, "It is finished" (John 19:30). He had borne the full weight of our sin and paid its full penalty.

As remarkable as that is, there is more to the story. Paul goes on to write that God "made him to be sin who knew no sin, so that in him we might become the righteousness of God" (2 Cor. 5:21 ESV). Not only were our sins counted to Jesus, but Jesus's own righteousness was counted to us. This means that righteousness—right standing with God—is a gift we receive, not a reward that we earn. Righteousness before God is not something that we merit but rather something that Christ has merited for us and bestowed graciously and freely on us.

The Greek word that is translated as "righteousness" is also translated as "justification." Paul uses this word frequently in his letters. He tells the Corinthians that "Christ . . . became to us wisdom from God, righteousness and sanctification and redemption" (1 Cor. 1:30 ESV). He told the Romans that the gospel reveals the righteousness of God, going on to say that we are justified by faith in Jesus Christ in just the same way that Abraham was justified (see Rom. 4:1–3)—namely, by faith in God. Justification is a gift we receive through faith in God and what he has done; it is not the achievement of the highly spiritual but rather the astonishing gift that God gives to the undeserving and broken.

Paul so emphasizes that this gift of righteousness is free, undeserved, and given by love that he eliminates every human achievement, religious observance, ethnic pedigree, or social standing as potential criteria for being part of God's family. Even though we were born into a fallen household, a rebellious family that was named for Adam and Eve, Jesus has paid the full penalty of that rebellion against God. Not only does God declare us to be utterly and completely free from any guilt associated with the human fall and our sinful condition and actions, but he goes even further and counts Jesus's own perfect righteousness to us. Then he goes further than that and says that we are sons of God through faith in Jesus Christ. In other words, God adopts us as his own children.

This is why the Holy Spirit is referred to as the "Spirit of adoption" and why we cry out from the depths of our being, "Abba! Father!" (Rom. 8:15). Like the little boy who was running up and down the aisle of the airliner, we celebrate with great joy and delight the love that God has for us as his children. This freely given status is bestowed on us by grace, in Jesus, making us the children of the living God.

THE GREATEST LOVE

"See what kind of love the Father has given to us, that we should be called children of God; and so we are" (1 John 3:1 ESV). Sadly, many Christians have not yet fully embraced this amazing truth. So many people who go by the label *Christian* try to earn favor with God, try to do things that they believe will somehow make God love them more—when in fact nothing they do could make him love them any less or any more than he always has and does. God has loved us eternally, sacrificially, and supremely in the gift of his son Jesus Christ. Even when we run away from him, our status as his children remains unchanged. We are the children of the living God, and he is our Abba Father—whether we are at our best or at our worst. J. I. Packer wrote, "If you want to judge how well a person understands Christianity, find out how much he makes of the thought of being God's child, and having God as his Father."[1] He's absolutely right, of course.

Some people don't have a deep experience of the fatherhood of God—and thus of their own belovedness in his sight—because they've had difficult, even diabolical, experiences with their fathers.[2] The pain and the wounds of contemptible treatment create scars that mark their lives for years. Even the best of human fathers is imperfect and will make mistakes in judgment, decisions, and discipline. Not only that, but fatherhood is largely despised today, and many children grow up without a father in the home.

Against the backdrop of failed fatherhood, we have to remember that God's fatherhood for his children is absolutely perfect. Having God as our father means that we are loved perfectly and securely and eternally. Paul wrote that God gave us our destiny in Jesus Christ because of his love for us before time began. This means that God's love for us in no way depends on our performance or even on our response to him. He loved us when we did not love him. "We love because he

---

1. J. I. Packer, *Evangelical Magazine* 7, 19–20; quoted in *Knowing God* (1973; repr., Downers Grove, IL: Inter-Varsity Press, 1993) 201.

2. My own dad suffered deeply at the hands of his alcoholic and neglectful father, but he became in Christ a beloved child of God and a wonderful father to me.

first loved us" (1 John 4:19 ESV). The initiative is wholly with God, and it began before the first day ever dawned.

This means that we do not come before God with a résumé of our righteousness that will somehow endear us to him. Leave at the door any thought that your performance as a "good kid" could commend you to God; lay aside any fear that your failures will bar you from God's favor. Both are trash that needs to be taken out. We come running to God because he has already loved us perfectly, and that will never change—because he never changes.

That eternal, unchanging love brought God to our rescue through the sacrifice of Jesus Christ. God desires to root our lives in his love for us so that, liberated from any kind of performance-based relationship, we instead enjoy the beauty and security of being his own sons and daughters who are loved perfectly—no matter how imperfectly we love or are loved by others. This relationship doesn't depend on some kind of righteousness that we have to earn. God's love in our lives is never a reward for a job well done—a certificate for us to hang on the walls of our conscience. Far from this, we live lives of joyful freedom, knowing that we are his children now and forever. Like the child running up and down the aisle in the airliner, we finally begin to joyfully celebrate life, because we are the Lord's.

Because we have been justified by grace through faith in Jesus Christ, we are adopted as God's own children, and his love for us will never let us go. The same love that he bestowed on us in Christ before time began, without any reference to anything we had done, remains ours because of our adoption as God's children. It does not depend on what we have done but depends only and exclusively on what Christ has done. We were chosen by God to be his children, and he has loved us to life in and through Jesus Christ.

I will never forget standing in a courtroom after having answered all the questions put to me by a judge about whether or not I understood and was willing to take up the responsibilities of being the father of my first child. The judge looked me in the eye and declared that the tiny baby boy was mine by adoption and that nothing could ever change that. He said, "Your marriage may even end, but your fatherhood of this boy can't and won't!" Though sobering, that moment was also one of inexpressible happiness.

The joy that I felt that day is but a distant echo of an eternally deeper joy in the heart of God the Father, who has done so much to secure us as his own beloved children. My friend, an even greater tribunal has been assembled for us, and a greater judge sits in the chair. The judge himself is the one adopting, and he is adopting not a single child but *all* those who have put their faith in Jesus. He vows to make them his own forever, and he places the Spirit of his Son Jesus in their hearts. The very name that Jesus uses in his relationship with God—*Abba*—is the name that he gives us to use as well.

A TALE OF TWO SONS

In one of Jesus's most famous stories, two sons respond to their father's love in two very different but identically fatal ways. An older brother faithfully labors with his father in his fields and is diligent to oversee all that belongs to his father, never missing a beat or failing in even one of the expectations that he believes his father has set before him. His younger brother despises his father and his household and decides to run as far away as he can to a distant land. He is the Prodigal Son—the one who is profligate with the inheritance that he demands and that the father yields to him. He takes the inheritance and gets as far away as he can from home and from the father he despises. Then, as Jesus tells the story, the son squanders that vast inheritance on riotous living—drunkenness, sexual immorality, and the like—until there is nothing left.

A terrible famine hits the land, and with no work available, he finds himself reduced to feeding swine. In that terrible, impoverished state, as he longs to eat the pigs' food, one of the most wonderful statements of Scripture appears: Jesus says that "he came to himself" (Luke 15:17 ESV). That is what happens when the Holy Spirit is at work in us: before we come to God, we come to ourselves. We face the lunacy of what we've done; we deal with the nightmare scenario that is our own soul. We see the destructiveness of our own actions, and we know that what we've done has led us to a place of utter desolation.

What happens next is so beautiful. This wayward son remembers his father's house. He knows that he needs to get home. But will he be welcomed back? That is the question.

He devises a scheme by which he might at least eat and quite possibly might work his way back into his father's favor by paying off the debt of the inheritance he had taken and so recklessly tossed aside. "I will arise and go to my father, and I will say to him, '. . . Treat me as one of your hired servants'" (Luke 15:18–19 ESV). Jesus tells us that the father, when he saw the wayward son returning home "while he was still a long way off, . . . ran and embraced him and kissed him" (v. 20 ESV). The loving father celebrated the homecoming of his son.

The boy began his well-rehearsed speech, asking to be made a hired man—but he was never able to finish it. "Quickly!" said the father. "Bring out the best robe, put sandals on his feet and a ring on his finger, and kill the fatted calf—we need to have a party for the prodigal. Let's celebrate! This son of mine who is dead is alive again" (see vv. 22–24).

It must have absolutely stunned that young man to

know that, inexplicably and unexpectedly, his father's love for him had never changed—despite the despicable way he had treated him. He would not have to earn his way back into the family; in fact, he could not earn his way back. Only grace and love could handle the weight of his debt. The father simply forgave it all and, in great love, celebrated his homecoming.

The older brother was unimpressed with this benevolence and refused to go into the party. When the father urged him to do so, the older son said to him, "This son of yours wasted your wealth, while I have been faithful to do everything you asked—yet you've never given me a party" (see vv. 29–30). The father looked with love on the older son and said to him, "All that is mine is yours" (v. 31). It has always been so—come to the party.

We don't know whether the older son ever went into the celebration. What we do know is that the father loved his sons—both the licentious son and the legalistic one. They both mistakenly thought they were in a performance-based relationship. One thought that he could escape his father by running as far away from him as he could, and then he thought that he would have to earn his way back into his good graces. The older son thought that by staying and being faithful he was somehow building up his résumé, earning the favor of his father, possibly increasing his father's love for him. Both these sons' false views of their father drove a wedge into their hearts. The younger could not wait to get away, and in the end the older one wanted to stay away.

Like the Prodigal Son, we are all a sinful mess, trashing our existence through our narcissistic abandonment of the good and beautiful in favor of the temporary high. The love of God the Father reaches out to us in our shame and wandering and rebellion and welcomes us home into his house, saying to us, "You cannot earn your place as my son. Your place as my child is a gift I have bestowed on you through my eternal and unchanging love." The love of God the Father reaches out to us in our self-righteousness and do-it-yourself salvation projects—the kinds of things we do so that God will owe us a party. The father says to all of us in our self-righteousness, "My love for you is as free and unearned as it is undeserved; my love for you is a gift that I bestow richly, abundantly, and joyfully."

God the Father invites us as his adopted children, who have been liberated from a failed house of treason, to celebrate with him in the eternal and joyful feast that is the kingdom of heaven. All this is ours through Jesus Christ his Son, who bestows on us the Spirit, who in turn from our hearts cries out words to God that we never imagined could be ours: "Abba, Father."

FOR REFLECTION OR GROUP DISCUSSION

1. Look at Galatians 4:6 and discuss how the word *Abba* impacts your view of God and how you relate to him.

2. In the light of Ephesians 2:3 and I John 3:1–3, why is this so amazing?

3. Read Romans 8:14–15. Why is it impossible for our "adoption" and "justification" to be something we earn or merit?

4. Sometimes we view God's fatherhood through the lens of our experience of our very frail, and even sometimes terribly flawed and abusive, human fathers. How is God's fatherhood completely different from this human experience of fathering?

5. Read the parable of the two sons and their father in Luke 15. Discuss the differences between the two brothers. What was unchanging in the Father throughout his

approach to both sons? Do you identify most with the younger son or the older son? How might you imitate the Father and his love?

6. As a group, sing "Before the Throne of God Above" by Charitie Lees Bancroft.

9

UNION WITH CHRIST

The Indispensable Bond

By His doing you are in Christ Jesus.
—*Paul the Apostle*

Communion between God and man is the . . .
definition of Christianity.
—*J. I. Packer,* A Quest for Godliness

I'm so glad that my mom taught me to how to read long before I ever went to school. I'm also glad that my dad taught me what to read, starting with the *Peanuts* comic strip that showed up every day in this thing that people once read, long ago, called a newspaper. One of my favorites involves Charlie Brown sitting down at Lucy's Psychiatry Booth for some analysis. After dropping his required nickel into the can, Charlie begins to unpack his problem. Here's the gist of it.

"I feel depressed."

"Why is that, Charlie Brown?"

"Because I feel inferior."

This is when is gets good, because Lucy is so bad. "Don't feel badly about that, Charlie Brown. Lots of people feel that way," she opines.

"What? That they feel inferior?"

"No," Lucy says—"they feel that you're inferior!"

Ouch. We can feel the dagger go in. And yet we laugh. Why? At one level, we're amused by Lucy's clever use of the language; but, more importantly, we probably laugh a little defensively—we are all Charlie Brown, and we suspect that Lucy is confirming the darkest fears that we harbor about ourselves and how others see us. How we wish we could be other than the people we are; how often we've wanted to be at the cool kids' table but weren't.

We can attempt to overcome our status envy and social insecurity through analysis, wealth accumulation, or the pursuit of power and pleasure. The wisest king of the ancient world tried that and concluded that it was "vanity and a striving after wind" (Eccl. 1:14 ESV)—a poetic way of saying, "That dog won't hunt." He also noted that God has placed eternity in the deep space of our hearts, where God's depths meet human souls. This is why we yearn to belong to the greater—to the eternal. We were made for a larger life and for communion, deep communion, with God.

JOINED TO JESUS

Much of the Christian teaching that I come across emphasizes forgiveness of sins and reconciliation with God—which is certainly the core message—but at the expense of the vital truth that God not only forgives us but also *unites us to himself in Jesus Christ*. John Calvin, one of the greatest Christian theologians of all time, wrote of union with Christ,

"As long as Christ remains outside of us and we are separated from him, all that he has suffered and done for the salvation of the human race remains useless and of no value to us. . . . He became ours to dwell within us."[1] That's an incredible assertion. What Jesus has done won't benefit us at all unless our lives are united to him. "Mystical union" with Christ, Calvin wrote, has "the highest importance."[2]

The idea of being united to Jesus is seen in the act of Christian baptism. In the ancient world, baptism wasn't simply a person's declaration of allegiance to another or a sign of cleansing. It was also a radical act of identification with and of joining to another. Baptism is always "into" someone.[3] When Jesus gave the Great Commission to his disciples, he told them to go and make disciples of all nations, baptizing them in the name of the Father and the Son and the Holy Spirit. Literally, that's baptizing them *into* the name of the Trinity.

Baptism by the Spirit and water initiates communion— *common union*—with God. In the rite of holy baptism, the Spirit unites people to Jesus Christ. This is why Paul writes to the Romans that we are buried with Christ through baptism into his death. Just as Christ was raised from the dead, so we too, through our union with him, might also be raised from the dead and walk in newness of life (see Rom. 6:4). Through the work of the Holy Spirit, those who believe in Jesus are united to him—in Paul's words, they are now in Christ, and Christ is in them.

1. John Calvin, *Institutes of the Christian Religion*, ed. John T. McNeill, trans. Ford Lewis Battles (Philadelphia: The Westminster Press, 1960), 3.11.10.

2. Calvin, 3.11.10.

3. This is clearly seen when Paul wrote that Israel was "baptized into Moses in the cloud and in the sea" (1 Cor. 10:2).

THE HOPE OF GLORY

Our relationship with Christ is one in which our lives are intertwined with his. Paul writes to the Colossians that "Christ in you" is "the hope of glory" (Col. 1:27); he also writes in numerous places that we are now "in Christ," and this new relationship—Christ in us and us in Christ—is absolutely essential to what it means to be a Christian. This deep, eternal joining together of Jesus Christ and his people is a postcard version of the gospel. Don't let its brevity obscure its beauty or significance.

Let's look at just a few examples of this kind of language:

If anyone is *in Christ*, he is a new creation. (2 Cor. 5:17 ESV)

He made Him who knew no sin to be sin on our behalf, so that we might become the righteousness of God *in Him*. (2 Cor. 5:21)

He chose us *in Him* before the foundation of the world, that we would be holy and blameless before Him. (Eph. 1:4)

You were dead in the trespasses and sins in which you once walked. . . . But God . . . made us alive together *with Christ* . . . and raised us up *with him* and seated us *with him* in the heavenly places *in Christ Jesus*. (Eph. 2:1–2, 4–6 ESV)

Paul goes on to use the language of union with Christ over one hundred thirty times in his ancient letters to the church. Theologians have long recognized this emphasis in Paul, noting how central it is to his understanding of what it means to be Jesus's disciple. Where did this understanding of salvation come from? How did Paul come to see that following Jesus meant being united to Jesus?

Perhaps one possibility is Paul's dramatic encounter with Jesus Christ on the road to Damascus. Paul, then called Saul, was a violent opponent of the Christian faith. Not only did he approve of the killing of the first Christian martyr, Stephen, but he was on his way from Jerusalem to Damascus in order to arrest more of Jesus's followers so that they too would suffer a similar fate. While he was on the road to Damascus, the risen and reigning Savior appeared to him, blinding him with the brightness of his revelation and knocking him to the ground. "Saul, Saul, why are you persecuting me?" asked Jesus. "Who are you, Lord?" he asked in return. "I am Jesus, whom you are persecuting" (Acts 9:4–5 ESV).

No evidence suggests that Saul of Tarsus had ever encountered Jesus Christ before that moment. He hadn't been part of the mob or one of the religious leaders who had worked for Jesus's death. Nevertheless, Jesus said that Saul was persecuting him. How did Paul persecute Christ when he'd never met him, heard him, seen him, or touched him?

While Saul had not personally touched Jesus, he had violently touched those who were Jesus's followers. Jesus was saying to him, "If you persecute those who are mine, you persecute me. You can't touch them without touching me. These followers of mine are part of me—they are joined to me; we are inseparable. In as much as you do it to the least of these my brothers, you have done it unto me." Right from the start, Saul knew that Jesus's followers have been united to Jesus in a bond that transcends time and space—one that can never be broken. His heart was converted to faith in Jesus, and he gave the rest of his life to telling others the good news about his Savior and Lord.

Later, Paul used the image of the human body to

describe to the Corinthian church what it meant for them to follow Jesus. Christ is the Head, and his church is the body. The Head and the body are joined together in such a way that the life of the body, and its direction, come from its Head— the Lord Jesus himself. Not only that, but every member of the body is vitally important, even if some members of the body tend not to think so highly of themselves, on the one hand, or too highly of themselves, on the other (see 1 Cor. 12:12–27). To be joined to Jesus is to be joined to other believers. We are united together in Christ.

But this joining of the Head and the body together in Christ is not something that belongs only to the church as a whole entity. When Paul talks about being joined to Jesus, he has in view each and every individual believer. And it isn't just our souls or our hearts that are united to Christ; rather, it is the entirety of our person, including our bodies. The foundation of Paul's Christian sexual ethics is rooted in union with Christ. Because our bodies are joined to Christ, they must not be joined to anyone else through any kind of immoral sexual relations. The joining of our bodies to Jesus through union with him is also the basis of our ultimate resurrection from the dead. Because the spirit of Christ dwells in our bodies, God will raise us from the dead in the same way that he raised Jesus himself from the dead, through the power of the Holy Spirit (see Rom. 8:11).

I sometimes hear people say, "I have given my heart to Jesus," and of course I rejoice when I hear them say so—but I always want to follow up on that profession of faith by urging those who say it to make sure that they give their bodies as well as their hearts. Our eyes belong to Jesus; our ears belong to Jesus; our tongues belong to Jesus; our hands and our feet belong to Jesus. Every single aspect of who we are has been redeemed by Jesus Christ through his death and resurrection.

The assertion that "it's my body and I can do with it whatever I want" is completely antithetical to the teaching of the New Testament. Paul writes that we are not our own, that we cannot do with our bodies just anything that we please, because we have been bought with a price—the precious blood of Jesus Christ—and joined to him, body and soul (see 1 Cor. 6:15–20).

One of the great creedal documents of the Reformation opens with a profoundly beautiful question and answer.

What is your only comfort in life and death?

That I, with body and soul, both in life and death, am not my own, but belong unto to my faithful Savior Jesus Christ.[4]

No aspect of our humanity has been left untouched or unreached by the magnificent scope of Jesus's love for us. Jesus comes to save not merely our souls but our bodies as well, and this is why we offer to him every aspect of who we are—spirit, soul, and body. Our bodies are temples of the Holy Spirit (see 1 Cor. 6:19). They are sacred spaces that are filled with the presence of the living God. Our minds are sacred spaces that are meant to be filled with the truth of God, and every moment of our existence, now and for all eternity, is filled with the life-giving presence of God himself.

While our justification depends not on anything that God does inside us but instead on what Jesus has accomplished in history, it is nevertheless true that all the benefits of what Jesus has done for us are communicated to us through the Holy Spirit as he works in us and applies to us that great work of Jesus.

---

4. Heidelberg Catechism, question and answer 1.

FROM DEATH TO LIFE

A young man came to my office one afternoon and told me that the only way forward for his life was to end it. He said that he had made such an absolute disaster of life that he had no hope of sorting it out. "I need to just die," he said.

"You're right," I said, looking at him. "Death is the only way out for you."

Needless to say, he was shocked. "What do you mean?" he cried.

"I mean," I replied, "that our lives, left to their own devices and not lived for the glory of God, will only take us down a path that leads to death. God knows this, which is why he offers us an entirely new life in union with Jesus Christ. Through the Holy Spirit, our lives come to an end, and Jesus's own life begins to shine through ours. Not only is the guilt of our sin transferred to Christ and the righteousness of Christ transferred to us, but God gives the very life of Jesus Christ to us, transforming us and giving us an entirely new status and identity in Christ. God isn't offering you a second chance; he's offering you a whole new life. That's the promise of the gospel, made by the one who 'makes all things new.'"

Paul highlights this radical new life and status in his letter to the Galatians when he writes, "I have been crucified with Christ; and it is no longer I who live, but Christ lives in me; and the life which I now live in the flesh I live by faith in the Son of God, who loved me and gave Himself up for me" (Gal. 2:20). Coming alive to faith in Jesus means coming to an end of life on our own terms. This is why we are baptized into the death of Jesus Christ: "we have been buried with Him through baptism into death" (Rom. 6:4). Following that death and burial, we are also raised to life through Jesus Christ and given an entirely new kind of life in which we are "no longer

... slaves to sin" (Rom. 6:6) but instead "in Christ Jesus ... are all sons of God, through faith" (Gal. 3:26 ESV).

ALL OF CHRIST FOR ALL OF LIFE

Our being united to Christ, in body and soul, means that we can affirm five vital truths.

We Have an Entirely New Identity

Prior to becoming a follower of Jesus, Saint Augustine lived a life that was characterized by sexual adventure and a considerable amount of partying. He had many lovers, a mistress, and a son born out of wedlock—nothing about his life showed any interest in anything other than the pursuit of pleasure and fame. A popular tale has it that on one occasion after his conversion to faith in Jesus, a former lover crossed his path and was surprised to see that, rather than stopping and speaking to her and perhaps even trying to seduce her, Augustine kept walking. She turned and pursued him and, confronting him, said, "Augustine, it is I." "Yes," said Augustine, "but it is not I."[5]

Augustine was rightly aware that his old life had passed away and a new life had begun; his identity was no longer the same, because he was now "in Christ." Whereas once he would have been counted only as a sinner, he was now a saint called by God as one of his holy people—and this not because of anything he had done, but because he was now in Christ Jesus and Christ Jesus was in him. In the same way, you too have a new identity. It is no longer you who live but Christ who lives in you.

---

5. A story noted by many that is perhaps apocryphal but would be in keeping with his experience and wit.

This is the heart of Paul's beautiful words "If anyone is in Christ, he is a new creation. The old has passed away; behold, the new has come" (2 Cor. 5:17 ESV). It's also right at the heart of one of the most critical issues in our culture: the meaning of identity. New World culture largely rejected the notion of *assigned identity*, in which we are what our family says we are, in favor of *accomplishment identity*, in which we are what we achieve. Recently, however, people have moved away from this idea, noting that we are more than what we "do" and that our accomplishments cannot fully define us—as great as those achievements may be, they can also fade and be lost. In place of this is an *assertive identity* in which we are whatever we say we are. No one can define us; we define our own reality—even our gender and race—and no one can deny us the identity that we assert is our own. "You be You" is the only permitted response to the person who, knowing that he needs a new identity, asserts one of his own choosing.

The gospel negates the shortcomings of each of these three approaches while also embracing the truth each one claims. In union with Christ, we are *assigned* an identity as children of God; a gracious, *achieved* identity is bestowed on us in the gift of Christ's own righteousness, which is merited by him and freely given to us; and our identity is *asserted*—but by the one who alone can say, "I Am that I Am" (Ex. 3:14 KJV). When John the Baptist was asked, "Who are you . . . ? What do you say about yourself?" (John 1:22), he answered not by asserting his achievements or conforming to the expectations of those who asked him, but by quoting what God said about him in Isaiah: "I am a voice of one crying in the wilderness" (John 1:23). We find our identity in the grace of God, which joins us to the perfect life of Christ and makes of us a "new creation."

We Have an Entirely New Trajectory

When Christ is in you and you are in Christ, your life is no longer about your goals or aspirations but rather about the will of God. Paul says, "It is no longer I who live, but Christ lives in me; and the life which I now live in the flesh I live by faith in the Son of God" (Gal. 2:20). Writing to the Romans, he also says, "Do not be conformed to this world, but be transformed by the renewing of your mind" (Rom. 12:2). Before we were in Christ, we were left to live only for our own pleasures and passions, whatever they might have been. But now, in Christ, we have an entirely new purpose and mission. We live by faith in the Son of God, who loved us and gave himself for us. Our lives are shaped by the cross. We live for the glory of God and in subjection to the will of God. These become our new chief delight and joy.

We Have an Entirely New Ability

My friend Rankin Wilbourne has written an entire—and an entirely wonderful—book on union with Christ. In one of my favorite sections, Rankin suggests that being a Christian is a lot more like being Spider-Man than like being Batman. While the Caped Crusader is a wealthy guy with cool crime-beating gadgets, the Spider-Man has been transformed internally. "Spidey" was changed by a foreign entity that entered his system, permanently altering his DNA and giving him the ability to do things that others can't do—no matter how many cool tools they possess. A person who is united to Jesus has within her the ability of Jesus; the Spirit of God has not "draped" Jesus over us but joined us together with him in such a way that Christ is in us and we are in Christ. His life dwells in us.[6]

6. See Rankin Wilbourne, *Union with Christ: The Way to Know and Enjoy God* (Colorado Springs: David C Cook, 2016), 52–53.

The Scripture that was most quoted by the ancient church fathers is Jesus's statement "Apart from Me you can do nothing" (John 15:5). The early Christians knew that their ability to live by faith, to bring the news of Jesus to the farthest ends of creation, and to endure deep suffering—and even martyrdom—arose not from themselves but from the life of Jesus himself within them. The second-century Christian martyr Felicitas, a Roman citizen of high standing, gave birth to a child while in prison. Her guards taunted her, saying that if she cried out in pain as she was giving birth, what made her think she could endure being set on by wild beasts in the arena? Her answer was all about the strength of another. "Now I suffer what I suffer," she answered, referring to her labor pains; "then," referring to her approaching martyrdom, "another will be in me who will suffer for me, as I shall suffer for him."[7]

Where does our power to walk with, serve, and follow Jesus come from? Not from ourselves. We are weak, but "in him" we are made strong. We are dead, but "in him" we are alive. We are sinful, but "in him" we are righteous. The mystical union of believers with Jesus means that Jesus's own life is in us, changing us from the inside out and securing us, now and for all eternity, in communion with God.

We Have an Entirely New Community

The Holy Spirit baptizes us into the body of Christ—the church. Since I am united to Jesus, through the same spirit I am also united to all those in every place who also enjoy that relationship with Jesus. We are all, each and every one of us, members of his body—members of one another. Paul wrote

7. Philip Caraman, ed., *Saints and Ourselves* (New York: Doubleday, 1958), 20.

that Christ is the "head over all things to the church, which is His body, the fullness of Him who fills all in all" (Eph. 1:22–23). There's no room to approach the Christian faith in an entirely individualized way. While faith is always deeply personal, it is never exclusively personal—our faith is also always communal.

Faith does not simply bestow saving grace on sinful individuals and then leave us to struggle along on our own; it also unites us in a new community, the body of Christ. We become one with believers everywhere—and everywhen. We are united to the faithful Christians who went before us and are already in heaven; we are also with all those who are now living, regardless of their race, gender, social status, ethnicity, nationality, or denomination; and we are even with all who will come after us as the years roll on. This is what is meant by the phrase "the communion of the saints" in the Apostles' Creed. We believe that we have a shared communion, through Jesus Christ, with "all those who in every place call upon the name of our Lord" (1 Cor. 1:2 ESV). Faithful Christian living is done not in isolation but in joyous participation in the community of believers that Jesus called "my church."

Reflecting on the days immediately after his conversion to Christianity, C. S. Lewis notes that he did not find being part of the church something necessary or attractive, but that he later came to see the great value of being in communion with God's people. He wrote,

> My own experience is that when I first became a Christian, about fourteen years ago, I thought that I could do it on my own, by retiring to my rooms and reading theology, and I wouldn't go to the churches and Gospel Halls; and then later I found that it was the only way of flying your flag; and, of course, I found that this meant being a target.

. . . If there is anything in the teaching of the New Testament which is in the nature of a command, it is that you are obliged to take the Sacrament, and you can't do it without going to Church. I disliked very much their hymns, which I considered to be fifth-rate poems set to sixth-rate music. But as I went on I saw the great merit of it. I came up against different people of quite different outlooks and different education, and then gradually my conceit just began peeling off. I realized that the hymns (which were just sixth-rate music) were, nevertheless, being sung with devotion and benefit by an old saint in elastic-side boots in the opposite pew, and then you realize that you aren't fit to clean those boots. It gets you out of your solitary conceit.[8]

We Have an Entirely New Destiny

Jesus prayed to his Father that those whom the Father had given to him would be "with Me where I am" (John 17:24), and this prayer will surely be answered. Jesus will not suffer any member of his body to remain in the grave, any more than God the Father allowed Christ's physical body to remain in the grave two thousand years ago. The same Spirit of Holiness who raised Jesus from the dead outside Jerusalem will likewise raise our bodies from the dead and conform our new bodies to the resurrected body of Jesus. Whether the dead are in graves or in oceans, whether their bodies have been buried or consumed by fire, whatever form of decay their bodies have taken, and in whatever location they rest, the power of God will raise the bodies of believers from the dead and will conform them to the body of Jesus Christ in his glorious resurrection. We will be with him forever, just as he prayed.

---

8. C. S. Lewis, *God in the Dock: Essays on Theology and Ethics*, ed. Walter Hooper (Grand Rapids: Eerdmans, 1970), 51–52.

There's no aspect of our salvation that isn't related to this incredible joining to Jesus. We are elect—chosen "in Christ before the foundation of the world." We are justified and sanctified "in him." The life we now live is possible only because Christ is "in us." In the end, we will be glorified "through him."

I have officiated at countless weddings over the years, and I always look forward to two beautiful moments in particular. The first is when the groom sees his bride appear at the head of the aisle, ready to come down and be joined to him. At almost every wedding I've been privileged to perform, the groom has smiled broadly and often wept with joy at the sight of his beloved bride. The second moment is much like the first. Once the man and woman have shared their vows and exchanged their rings, they stand before me, and I say these words: "They are no longer two, but one flesh. What therefore God has joined together, let no man separate" (Matt. 19:6). In that moment, the two people are united in a bond that changes them forever.

Sadly, our unions in marriage are far too frequently broken. It is not so with the Lord. When he unites us to himself, he never breaks the bond. When the Bible calls us the bride of Christ and tells us that Jesus is our bridegroom, it reminds us that Christ is the faithful groom who rejoices over us because of the great love that he has for us, which caused him to give his very life for us in order to make us his own. He joins us to himself, uniting us in an eternal bond that can never be broken. When it comes to your relationship with Christ, you are now one with him—you are in Christ and Christ is in you, and what God has joined together, no one can pull apart.

FOR REFLECTION OR GROUP DISCUSSION

1. Being a Christian means that you are in Christ and Christ is in you. Discuss how this changes your view of God's nearness and his relationship to you.

2. Read this quote from John Calvin, and discuss the benefits that we have because we are in Christ: "As long as Christ remains outside of us and we are separated from him, all that he has suffered and done for the salvation of the human race remains useless and of no value to us. . . . He became ours to dwell within us."

3. How might Paul's encounter with Jesus on the Damascus Road have shaped his understanding of the body of Christ?

4. Talk about the implications of your body being in union with Christ. How does this impact your view of sexuality? Of service? Of violent speech or behavior?

5. Discuss how 2 Corinthians 5:17 speaks to the issue of our identity.

6. Read Romans 12:1–2 and discuss how union with Christ reshapes our view of living for God in this world.

7. How do you view the reality of Christ's life dwelling in you?

8. How does union with Christ affect your view of being in a church family?

9. Union with Christ impacts our view of the future. How would you describe your future as a member of Christ's people?

10. As a group, sing "In Christ Alone" by Keith Getty and Stuart Townend.

10

SPIRITUAL CONFLICT
The Indispensable Fight

I won't back down.
—Song by Tom Petty

Our struggle is not against flesh and blood, but . . .
against the spiritual forces of wickedness.
—Paul the Apostle

Battlefields are compelling places to visit. Whether the Little Bighorn in Montana, the vast expanse of grass and trees at Shiloh, a forest outside Bastogne in Belgium, or the beaches of Normandy, such locations remind us not only of the great tragedy of human violence but also of great courage displayed in the face of a powerful enemy. For love and honor, for a cause greater than themselves, people were willing to lay down their lives—and they changed history. Our society is shaped by monumental battles, not just by great ideas and inventions. From Marathon to Midway, from Gettysburg to

Golgotha, the world has changed because someone fought the good fight.

It may surprise you to think of Christians as living on a battlefield, but that is the way that Scripture portrays us. Far from being called to an easy life, those who follow Jesus soon discover that they are engaged in an epic cosmic battle for their souls, for their neighbors, for their communities, and for the world. It's even fair to say that we not only *live* on a battlefield but also find ourselves at times to *be* the territory over which the warfare rages. John Newton, writer of the iconic hymn "Amazing Grace," wisely observed that sufferings and misfortunes—including our wrestling with temptations that arise from our own passions and from external powers—are typical for those who believe. In fact, these sufferings are designed and employed by Providence for the maturing of Christian disciples.[1] This is the fight of our lives—and it is indispensable.

WAKE UP!

I meet many people who are blissfully unaware that a spiritual battle rages around or within them—but I am always surprised when those people are Christians. After all, many passages of Scripture make plain that we really are in a spiritual battle. The following are but a few I could point out.

> Be on the alert. Your adversary, the devil, prowls around like a roaring lion, seeking someone to devour. (1 Peter 5:8)

1. There are a host of passages to illustrate this view in Newton, and the entirety of his work is beneficial. Please see *The Letters of John Newton* (Monergism Books), *The Works of John Newton* (Banner of Truth), and, for a more accessible approach, *Newton on the Christian Life* by Tony Reinke (Crossway).

Our struggle is not against flesh and blood, but . . . against the spiritual forces of wickedness. . . . Therefore, take up the full armor of God. (Eph. 6:12–13)

By the weapons of righteousness for the right hand and the left . . . (2 Cor. 6:7)

I have fought the good fight. (2 Tim. 4:7)

To the one who conquers I will grant to eat of the tree of life. (Rev. 2:7 ESV)

My brother Steve is a warrior. Literally. He's a big guy and a larger-than-life character, and even though he's my "little brother" I have looked up to him for years. That's not only because he's about three inches taller than I am, but because his heart for serving his country is so proud and sacrificial. He served for many years in the US Navy Explosive Ordnance Disposal, which means he was in some very dangerous places indeed. Not only is he an expert on explosives and trained in hand-to-hand combat, he is also able to set up and command security detail—and has done so for the highest officeholders in this country. He's big enough to be a shield, smart enough to outthink any enemy, and tough enough to outlast any ordeal. I'd invade hell with water pistols if Steve led the charge. You probably know people like Steve yourself—"hard men" who are on the walls so that we can sleep peacefully in our beds. Thank God for these warrior men and women.

One other thing about Steve needs to be noted, and it's true of all great warriors: he is under no illusions about the enemy. A civilian can afford to be ignorant of enemy capabilities, strategies, and intent; warriors can't afford that luxury. That's why the passages above are so important. If they are true—and they are—then there are no civilians in this king-dom; each and every one of us is a citizen-soldier. Being a Christian means being engaged in a conflict that's been raging since the dawn of time. The stakes are immeasurably high, the casualties are real, and there aren't any "reserves" who can join us—we're all active forces. Don't think for a second that you can ignore this conflict. The church is a battleship, not a cruise liner; so buckle up, strap in, and get ready to take your place in the greatest force ever assembled.

THE DARK SIDE

I get it if you doubt all this talk about a supernatural foe or find it hard to believe in angels and devils. Here, again, the great teacher C. S. Lewis has some good advice: "There are two equal and opposite errors into which our race can fall about the devils. One is to disbelieve in their existence. The other is to believe, and to feel an excessive and unhealthy interest in them. They themselves are equally pleased by both errors and hail a materialist or a magician with the same delight."[2]

The Christian approach is to take the battle seriously, and to understand that our service and struggle are part of a conflict, but not to end up yielding territory to the enemy by doing what he most wants us to do: obsessing over him and fearing him. Martin Luther was under no illusions about the devil and his power, and he wrote of the battle with him in his memorable hymn "A Mighty Fortress is Our God."

> For still our ancient foe
> Doth seek to work us woe;

2. C. S. Lewis, *The Screwtape Letters* (repr., San Francisco: HarperOne, 2015), 9.

His craft and power are great,
And, armed with cruel hate,
On earth is not his equal.[3]

That isn't where he left things. The hymn goes on to say that while we can't trust in our own strength to conquer this foe, we can trust in the power of Christ: "He must win the battle." Jesus Christ is the Warrior-King who equips us for the fight—one that we are in for the rest of our days.

Martin Luther often said that, next to Scripture itself, the best weapon against the devil is good music—that the enemy hates music because he despises our joy.[4] We don't ignore the reality of spiritual warfare, but neither do we doubt the strength of the forces that are lined up on the side of faith, hope, and love. This is why, in one sermon, Luther wrote, "When sadness comes to you and threatens to gain the upper hand, then say, 'Come, I must play our Lord Jesus a song . . . for Scripture teaches me that he loves to hear joyful song and stringed instruments.' Strike the keys with a will, and sing out until those thoughts disappear, as David and Elisha did. If the devil returns . . . defend yourself and say, 'Get out devil, I must now sing and play unto my Lord Jesus!'"[5] We are joyful warriors.

---

3. Martin Luther, "A Mighty Fortress Is Our God," 1529; trans. Frederic H. Hedge, 1853.

4. On this topic, see Roland H. Bainton, *Here I Stand: A Life of Martin Luther* (New York: Abingdon-Cokesbury Press, 1951), 340–47. "Music is a fair and lovely gift of God. . . . Next after theology I give to music the highest place and the greatest honor. I would not exchange what little I know of music for something great. Experience proves that next to the Word of God only music deserves to be extolled as the mistress and governess of the feelings of the human heart. We know that to the devils music is distasteful and insufferable." Luther, quoted in Bainton, 341.

5. Ewald M. Plass, *What Luther Says* (repr., St. Louis: Concordia, 1986), 983.

The prophet Elisha was once surrounded by enemy forces that had been sent to arrest him. His servant, deeply alarmed by the troops that were commanding the hillside, was ready to panic. "Open his eyes, Lord; show him that there are more with us than against us!" was Elisha's simple prayer. Suddenly his servant saw what had been veiled to him only moments beforehand: all around the opposing forces were thousands of angels (see 2 Kings 6:14–17).

The early Christians viewed the world in the same terms. Opposition? Certainly. But, they confessed, "greater is He who is in you than he who is in the world. . . . This is the victory that has overcome the world—our faith" (1 John 4:4, 5:4). When the apostles started preaching, the Roman landscape was marked by crosses. The same thing was true hundreds of years later—with one incredible difference. No longer were people dying on crosses by the thousands; now crosses were on the tops of buildings as emblems of hope, healing, and hospitality. The world had changed, and the darkness had been pushed back.

The ancient Christians expected the world to change, because the balance of power had decisively shifted. With the arrival of Jesus Christ, the battle had entered a new and decisive phase, and the victory that he won in the conflict of the cross defeated dark powers, delivered broken people from the guilt and grip of sin, and liberated everyone who was enslaved to the power of death.

As we continue in this chapter, we will explore Jesus's life and mission in terms of his confrontation with and triumph over the dark forces and will explore how, as the Champion-King representing us, he fought the fight and overcame every temptation. His example is critical because the weapons that he deployed are completely counterintuitive. Christ won through speaking, praying, dying, serving, and loving; he conquered pride through humility and overcame violent hate through mercy and kindness. This is why the people of Jesus "conquered [the accuser] by the blood of the Lamb and by the word of their testimony, for they loved not their lives even unto death" (Rev. 12:11 ESV). The Lion of the tribe of Judah, the great Warrior-King, is also the Lamb who sacrifices his life in love for his people.

JESUS OUR CHAMPION

In "A Mighty Fortress," Luther speaks of Jesus as "Lord Sabaoth"—a title that means "Lord of Hosts" and refers to Jesus's command of the heavenly army of holy angels. The holy angels are God's servants—and ours. When he was arrested, Jesus told those who were trying to defend him with man-made weapons that, if he wanted, he could summon ten thousand angels to help him to escape. The angels who had announced his birth to shepherds outside Bethlehem would have gladly rescued him from Gethsemane. Jesus chose a different approach to the battle. He went alone.

This wasn't the first time that Christ had confronted the powers of darkness. After his baptism, at the very beginning of his ministry, Jesus went into the wilderness of Judea and fasted there for forty days. In his weakened state, he was approached by Satan and tempted in three ways that were representative of all the temptations that befall humankind. In each case, Jesus threw back the Tempter, quoting God's Word as his weapon of defense. He three times cried, "It is written!" and banished the dark prince (see Matt. 4:1–11; Luke 4:1–13).

The first representative of humanity had succumbed to the seductive lies of the serpent in the garden of Eden and subjected himself, and all who proceed from him, to death. Thinking that he was buying power, Adam ended up with nothing but a cheap lie and a life of fear. Nevertheless, where Adam failed, Christ succeeded—resisting the devil as the head of a new humanity that would conquer the Tempter. Adam was in paradise with his beautiful bride, and he lost the fight; Christ was alone in a howling wilderness, hungry and thirsty, but he won.

Luke tells us that after his failed temptation Satan left Jesus "until an opportune time" (Luke 4:13)—a day that came three years later. Satan filled the heart of Judas Iscariot, one of Jesus's twelve chosen disciples, and he betrayed Jesus into the hands of the political powers that wanted him dead. An alliance between the Roman and religious powers saw to it that Jesus was killed on the cross. That's why, at the beginning of the chapter, I mentioned the battlefield of Golgotha. In everyone's eyes, that cross and that death looked like the defeat of Jesus that Satan had long sought to bring about. It wasn't.

Golgotha means "place of the skull." It was named as such, no doubt, because of the mass of human bones on that hill outside Jerusalem—all of which bore horrifying witness to Rome's ruthlessly efficient killing machinery. But there's more to it than that. When Adam first rebelled against God, thereby joining forces with the darkness, God spoke directly to the enemy and told him, in effect, "This means war!" God promised that one day a son would be born to a woman—a son who, while wounded in the battle, would "crush the head" of the serpent (Gen. 3:15).

The cross was a battlefield, and what looked like a defeat was, in fact, the greatest victory in history. At the cross, Paul wrote, God "[canceled] the record of debt that stood against us with its legal demands . . . nailing it to the cross" (Col. 2:14 ESV). But there was more. On the cross, the Son of God, the Warrior-King, confronted darkness and the devil. "He disarmed the rulers and authorities and put them to open shame, by triumphing over them" through the cross (Col. 2:15 ESV).

On Golgotha, the place of the skull, Jesus the Redeemer crushed the head of the serpent once and for all. The grand announcement of Jesus's victory that Friday night was made the following Sunday morning when he rose from the dead, liberating all who "through fear of death were subject to life-long slavery" (Heb. 2:15 ESV). Like David fighting Goliath for all the Israelites, Jesus the Son of David took on the ultimate threat and overthrew him—freeing forever, from guilt and the grave, all who put their trust in him.

THE BATTLE WITHIN

If Christ has defeated the devil on our behalf, why do we still struggle against him today? The Bible is very clear that we must take up the whole armor of God and stand against the schemes of the devil. Our enemy continues to fight, although he is on the retreat. Knowing that his doom is certain because of his defeat at Christ's hands, he does all that he can to inflict damage and woe until the final nail is in the coffin.

The devil is not our only enemy. Until our minds are completely renewed to God's truth, as revealed in Jesus Christ and in the Scriptures, our thoughts continue to be shaped and influenced by falsehood. In addition, the very passions of our body war against what we know to be God's will for our lives. Paul calls these "the deeds of the flesh" (Gal. 5:19), and they range from the prideful self-righteousness that religion some-times enthrones to the other end of the spectrum: the violent self-absorption that leads to anger, hatred, uncontrolled sexual desire, and the wounding not only of our own souls but of the people around us. Every single Christian faces a battle within, and it humbles us. Every day we awaken seeking to live lives that please God and to direct our hearts and minds in his ways. We nevertheless experience contrary impulses, and we wish that these could be tamed. What are we to do when the battle rages both without *and* within?

First, remember this key truth: Jesus has on our behalf defeated the powers of darkness, and his victory is counted as our own. As we saw in the last chapter, we are in union with Christ, and his triumph over temptation is now ours. We sometimes feel ashamed of our temptations and our sinful failures. When that's the case, we need to be reminded that Jesus experienced the same temptations when he became like us. The book of Hebrews says that Jesus "had to be made like his brothers in every respect, so that he might become a merciful and faithful high priest in the service of God, to make propitiation for the sins of the people. For because he himself has suffered when tempted, he is able to help those who are being tempted" (Heb. 2:17–18 ESV). Later we read that "we do not have a high priest who cannot sympathize with our weaknesses, but One who has been tempted in all things as we are, yet without sin" (Heb. 4:15). In our Savior, we find someone who knows our temptations. He comes not to judge and expose us but to renew and rescue us. This means that even when we fall—no, *especially* when we fall—we turn to the only one who can save us. Through him, we rise from the ashes of our defeats and find hope again.

A young man once asked me to pray that he would never be tempted by sin again. He was a very young Christian, his conscience was tender, and he was deeply grieved over the sins in his heart and the power and attraction they held for him. He longed to be delivered from them. I suggested that we pray together, so we took hands, and I said, "Oh Lord, this young man does not want to face temptation anymore. Please end his life today and take him to heaven. Amen."

Of course, he pulled his hands from mine and looked at me in the most shocked way you can imagine. "How can you possibly pray such a thing?" he exclaimed with real anger.

I think you can imagine what I told him. It brought a smile to his face, because he understood that even in his weakness he was seeing the power of Jesus Christ. The only time we will be absolutely free from temptation is when we leave this life—when our spirits and souls and bodies are made completely new in the presence of God with Jesus Christ. Until that day, we are in for the battle of our lives, and we must daily put on the whole armor of God and take up the shield of faith and the sword of the spirit. We must believe the gospel—that God forgives all our sins and will lead us by his Spirit to put to death more and more all those things in our lives that displease him.

We cannot do this in our own strength; we must do it by the power of the Holy Spirit. As he works in us through God's grace, we more and more come to delight in the things in which Jesus delights and reject those things that Jesus calls dangerous. This doesn't mean that we look like super spiritual champions of holiness at all times. In fact, this ongoing process of growth in holiness, which the Bible refers to as *sanctification*, remains incomplete in this life. It is most manifest by our growth in humility. The most mature believers (the most holy believers, if you will) are those who are most deeply aware of their need for a Savior—who sense most keenly their deep dependence on Jesus Christ. It is in this dependence on Jesus that we ultimately find the way to victory in the great battle of our lives.

LET GO AND LET GOD? NO!

Depending on Jesus doesn't mean that we aren't in the fight. Far from it. We are standing—and, as the late, great rocker Tom Petty put it so well, even up against the gates of hell we "won't back down." This isn't a "let go and let God" approach. Every day we engage with Scripture and with the reality of our own brokenness, all while firmly believing the gospel: that Christ has forgiven our sins and counts us as righteous in his sight.

With that settled, we know that whatever fallenness remains within us can be attacked by the Spirit and the Scriptures. Because we are seated with Christ in the heavenly places (see Eph. 2:6)—a new position—we can learn to walk in wisdom, light, and love. Because Christ is our shield and defense, we can stand in his grace, knowing that every single enemy we currently face or will ultimately confront must in the end bow its knee to Jesus Christ. We may fail repeatedly, but we never make peace with our enemy. The only peace we are interested in is the peace of Christ that is given through the gospel, reigns in our hearts, and is offered to all who believe. We work out our salvation, because we know that it is "God who is at work in [us], both to will and to work for His good pleasure" (Phil. 2:13).

How can we know that our history isn't our destiny? Paul wrote to his friends in Philippi that he was confident that what God had started in them he would perfect unto the day of Jesus Christ (see Phil. 1:6). God never brings us halfway home; he never starts things and leaves them unfinished. God "perfects" things—he brings to fruition and fullness all that he sets his hand to accomplish. Being conformed to Jesus's likeness is, in fact, the destiny to which we have been ordained. It's going to happen—not because we're so determined but because God is so faithful.

Let us not be discouraged as we encounter the array of temptations that ceaselessly rise from within us, the trials that descend upon us, and the attacks that frequently assault us.

We can "consider it all joy" (James 1:2)—largely because, if we don't meet the devil on the drive in to work, it may be because we are headed the same direction he is. Following after Jesus is certain to cause some head-on collisions with the darkness.

Fear not. Sometimes we will seem to do nothing but lose, but the ultimate victorious outcome has already been secured, and the day of dancing isn't that far off. In the end, Christ will conform us to his image in every possible way through the resurrection, will renew creation, and will eternally annihilate death and the devil. We will see this great final triumph in person and will join the victory procession that will never end. In the words of a great hymn, "We'll join the everlasting song and crown him Lord of all!"[6]

FOR REFLECTION OR GROUP DISCUSSION

1. In what ways have you recognized spiritual conflict going on in you and around you?
2. When you hear the word *devil*, what images spring to your mind? Do you think these are biblical images?
3. C. S. Lewis wrote, "There are two equal and opposite errors into which our race can fall about the devils. One is to disbelieve in their existence. The other is to believe, and to feel an excessive and unhealthy interest in them. They themselves are equally pleased by both errors and hail a materialist or a magician with the same delight." Which of these two errors are you more likely to fall into, and why?
4. Read Ephesians 6:10–18. With whom does Paul say that we "wrestle"? Against whom do we *not* wrestle? What

6. Edward Perronet, "All Hail the Power of Jesus' Name," 1780; lyrics revised by John Rippon, 1787.

are the various parts of "the armor of God"? Discuss what these various armaments are and what they do.

5. Read Matthew 4:1–11. In what ways does Jesus act as your representative champion as he overcomes Satan's temptations in the wilderness? What does this mean in terms of your own victory in this battle?

6. Hebrews 2 tells us that Jesus comes to our aid when we are tempted. How does he do so? What are our common temptations, and what help should we be looking for when we face such onslaughts?

7. As a group, sing "A Mighty Fortress Is Our God"!

11

SACRAMENTS

The Indispensable Mystery

[Abraham] received . . . a sign, a seal of the
righteousness that he had by faith.
—Paul the Apostle

Words are just not good enough to express
our experience of reality.
—Alister McGrath, Mere Theology

"It's a sign!" Recurring at key moments throughout the
late Nora Ephron's date-night movie *Sleepless in Seattle*, this little phrase draws us in to the "magic" that occurs at the intersection of people, circumstances, and hopes. From a tear in
a wedding dress to heart-shaped lights on the Empire State
Building, "It's a sign!" lets us know that the characters are being
carried along by more than mere logic. There is a mystery to
enter, a communion of souls to enjoy, and a great unfolding
purpose to try to understand. The signs point the way.

That's what signs do. They point beyond themselves and provoke us to take note, to pay attention, and to enter into the things we can't fully grasp with our limited intellects. Signs say, "There is more here than meets the eye." Without speaking, they whisper, "I'm trying to tell you something. Listen. See. Give attention."

READ THE SIGNS!

Beware. Exit. STOP. Enter.

We appreciate signs, and just about any facility manager will tell you that good signage is critical to order and productivity—anywhere from a college campus to an IT factory. If the signs aren't clear, people lose their way. It's hardly surprising, then, that God employs "good signage" in our lives to get his message through to us. It's not as though we are lacking access to God's message to us in plain language, because the Bible provides this—but putting certain signs before our senses brings the word of Scripture back to our minds; the sign points beyond itself and shows us the way toward having a deeper grasp of the words of Scripture in our souls.

We use the word *sacrament* to describe this language of signs. It's an English-language form of an old Latin word, *sacramentum*, which translates a Greek word used in the New Testament—one that is usually translated from Greek into English as "mystery." The sacraments are the holy mysteries of the church—the sign language of heaven that we can see and touch and hear and smell and taste. They reach aspects of our interior lives that are difficult to pin down. A good sermon that is delivered in the power of the Spirit reaches us with the gospel; sacraments have a similar mission, though they differ in the journey they take to reach us. The sermon's message goes for the heart via the head, but sacraments go straight for the heart via touch and taste.

The sacraments don't have power in themselves, any more than any sign conveys power. Yet these signs do have a unique relationship to the power that they point to. If I see a sign that reads "Danger" and has a radiation emblem on it, I avoid the area. The sign isn't dangerous, but it alerts me to the presence of a power I'd best give attention to. Baptism and the Lord's Supper, while signs, are also seals—meaning that they apply the power of what they signify to our lives, through the agency of the Holy Spirit. No power in the signs does the work, but the Spirit employs the signs to convey to us the very gifts that the signs speak of.

God speaks through the beautiful language of the signs. He is the one who creates water and then speaks over its surface, "Let there be light" (Gen. 1:3). He is the one who offers bread and wine to his disciples and says, "This is my body. . . . This is my blood. . . . Do this in remembrance of me" (see Mark 14:22–24; Luke 22:18–20; 1 Cor. 11:23–25). Signs are first and foremost God's voice communicating his love and covenant promise to us—the voice of a parent speaking to a child who doesn't comprehend the words but whose heart is united to the parent through the tenderness of the voice. Some people want to make the signs—and especially baptism—primarily about what we are saying about God ("I am now Christ's disciple"), but we need to bear in mind that, first and foremost, baptism concerns what God says about us ("This one is mine!"). After all, "We love, because He first loved us" (1 John 4:19).

The two sacraments that Jesus instituted are baptism and the Lord's Supper (which is sometimes called Communion or Eucharist). Both of them figure prominently in our worship and our life together as Christians. Let's briefly consider each and make sure we are on the receiving end of these great mysteries.

CHRISTIAN BAPTISM

In a wonderful scene in the George Clooney film *O Brother, Where Art Thou?* three escaped convicts happen on a public revival service. One of them, Delmar, races into the river to be baptized. Emerging from the water, he exclaims, "All my sins is washed away, includin' that Piggly Wiggly I knocked over in Yazoo," to which one of his companions responds, "I thought you said you was innocent of those charges!" Delmar barely misses a beat: "Well, I was lying. And . . . that sin's been washed away, too."[1] In Carrie Underwood's wise words, there was clearly "something in the water."

When, at a baptism, we see water wash over a person's head or entire body, we immediately think of the water's cleansing power. That's as it should be, because baptism speaks of our need for cleansing from sin. The waters of baptism represent the cleansing power of the blood of Jesus Christ. By receiving Christian baptism, people acknowledge their need for such cleansing—their absolute dependence on the mercy of God that is offered to them in the gospel and secured for them at the cross. "Wash away your sins," one disciple of Jesus told the newly converted Saul of Tarsus, referring to his need for Christian baptism (Acts 22:16). In a certain sense, Delmar got it right—when he emerged from the waters of baptism, his sins had been wiped away.

It isn't the water itself that cleanses us but rather the power that is beyond the sign. The Holy Spirit applies the

---

1. "Redemption," *O Brother, Where Art Thou?* directed by Joel Coen (2000; Burbank, CA: Touchstone Home Video, 2001), DVD.

cleansing that our souls need, and the cleansing agent is the blood of Christ. Through the direct agency of the Holy Spirit, Jesus's work in history is made real in our lives, and the use of water picks up on this reality. Over and over again, Scripture speaks of the Spirit in terms of water. He is referred to as a fountain that never runs dry, as a spring and a well, and even as a great river that flows and gives life to all. So when we see the sign of water administered in the name of the Father and the Son and the Holy Spirit, we are reminded that it is through the Holy Spirit that we have life. Nothing is more fundamental to life than water, and it is the water of the Holy Spirit that we most desperately need.

We've already seen that our sins can be forgiven only through Jesus Christ's atoning sacrifice. Baptism helps us to see our need for this cleansing. Our sins are "washed away" in baptism—not by the water itself but by what the water represents: the shed blood of Jesus Christ.

From the time of Abraham onward, the Jewish people have circumcised male infants in a rite that designates them as members of their community. Baptism works in similar ways. Baptism is the front door of the church. Whether it is received in infancy or later in life, it admits us to membership in the public community of God's people. Obviously not everyone who is baptized, whether in infancy or in adulthood, lives out a faithful Christian life; some even abandon and deny the faith altogether. Yet all who are baptized are acknowledged to be members of the church—not because of their own profession of faith, which may occur in baptism, but rather because in baptism God's profession of his promise over them in the gospel is most clearly heard and seen.

Paul says that Christian baptism is a new type of circumcision: a "circumcision made without hands" (Col. 2:11)—something that is done in the heart. In the setting of baptism, the Holy Spirit is secretly and mysteriously at work in the heart of the person being baptized. Obviously, the work of the Spirit is not confined to that moment. The Spirit's work may occur long before the baptism, and it may occur long after the baptism as well. Through baptism, however, the person is identified with the Christian community. All the promises that are made to believers are offered in baptism to the person who is being baptized.

While baptism is offered to adults, it must never be confined to them. It's not our age but our position in the covenant that determines that we should be baptized. This is why Peter told the thousands of people who were listening to his sermon in Jerusalem on the day of Pentecost, "Repent and be baptized every one of you in the name of Jesus Christ for the forgiveness of your sins, and you will receive the gift of the Holy Spirit. For the promise is for you and for your children" (Acts 2:38–39). In the book of Hebrews we read that our covenant in Christ is better, and comes with better promises, than the previous arrangements in the Bible (see Heb. 8:6). Since the old covenant included children, it's impossible to imagine that the new covenant—with its better promises—would be narrower in scope and would exclude children. Children are members of the covenant community, and Jesus's own teaching brought them into its center. When asked who was the greatest in the kingdom, Jesus took a child and set him in the midst of the crowd and said, "Whoever then humbles himself as this child, he is the greatest in the kingdom of heaven" (Matt. 18:4). The kingdom belongs to such as these.

What marks a person as a member of the covenant community? It is no longer circumcision but baptism. When a person becomes a Christian in adulthood, he should be baptized if he's never been baptized before. Those who are Christians should also bring their children to be baptized, thereby designating them as members of the Christian community—for that is what they are—and promising to raise them in the faith.

Jesus said that we are to go into all the world and "make disciples of all the nations, baptizing them in the name of the Father and the Son and the Holy Spirit, teaching them to observe all that I commanded you" (Matt. 28:19–20). Please notice that baptism is the very first thing that happens in the disciple-making process, because it designates a person as a follower of Jesus. Disciples then go on to be taught to embrace and follow Jesus's instruction for the rest of their lives.

In baptism, we hear God say over the baptized, "You are mine!" We also hear the church say to the baptized, "You're one of us!" This is why the rite of baptism is so important as a designation of who Jesus's disciples are. If you have not yet been baptized and you wish to identify yourself as a follower of Jesus, I urge you to "get up and be baptized . . . calling on [God's] name" (Acts 22:16), knowing that your sins are forgiven through the sacrificial offering of Jesus Christ, which the waters of baptism announce to you.

WELCOME TO THE FEAST

I confess to being something of a foodie. I love to cook—especially complex dishes that are prepared with French techniques or big Italian-style dinners with loads of pasta, home-baked fresh bread, and amazing sauces and charcuterie. I can't think of anything more fun than cooking for my family and friends or taking a series of classes at The Culinary Institute of America. There's something altogether wonderful about preparing a beautiful feast for the people you love and offering it to them. A good meal can help people to reconnect with each other and with the beauty that God has given to our world. There's no room in my house more important to me than the kitchen and no piece of furniture more important than our table.

In some ways, feasting and food are at the very center of the Bible's story of our redemption. This goes all the way back to creation. In the book of Genesis, we read that God made men and women in his image and placed Adam and Eve in a garden, surrounding them with every kind of nourishing thing to eat. God invited them to eat from every part of the garden, with the exception of the Tree of the Knowledge of Good and Evil. So humans were created to be creatures of feasting, and by eating and drinking—and by *not* eating—Adam and Eve were to show themselves to be faithful children of God.

This stands in stark contrast to pagan accounts of the origins of humanity. While the Bible describes God's creating food for us and stooping to provide for us, the ancient pagan myths approach things very differently. Let me cite but one example. In the Akkadian creation myth, the god Marduk, having crushed the skull of his rival god Tiamat, still has a problem with the other gods: they are hungry. Marduk takes Tiamat's remains and from them fashions humans, who are made to be servants of the gods so they can eat. "I will bring together blood and form bone, I will bring into being . . . 'man.' I will create . . . man on whom the toil of the gods will be laid that they may rest. . . . Let him establish lavish food offerings for his fathers, let him provide for their maintenance and be caretaker of their sanctuaries."[2] In this story, humans exist to satisfy the hunger of the gods; in the biblical account, God creates hungry humans and then serves them by providing for them all that they need.

2. *Enuma Elish* (The Babylonian Epic of Creation), trans. W. G. Lambert, in *Imagining Creation*, ed. Markham J. Geller and Mineke Schipper (Boston: Brill, 2007), 52, 54; available online at http://www.etana.org/node/581.

God gave Adam and Eve so many beautiful gifts, but they rebelled against him and ate the forbidden fruit. This act of defiance led to their exile from God's presence and from the beauty of paradise. If the fall of humankind came through eating, then it really isn't surprising that the message of redemption is put before us in a meal. The longest continually celebrated religious rite in the world is the feast of Passover, in which the Jewish people remember that God delivered them from the power of slavery and made them his own. God gave the Jews other feasts as well: the feasts of Pentecost and Tabernacles, as well as numerous opportunities to celebrate his goodness by eating and drinking the sacrifices that they brought into the temple. It was one way that people enjoyed communion with God.

While they were going through the wilderness on the way to the promised land, the Israelites needed food and water to sustain them. God gave them manna in the morning and water from the rock. He rescued his people through a shared meal. Much later in Israel's history, when the Jews faced annihilation at the hands of the Persian Empire, they were rescued through a series of five feasts that brought about the demise of the man who had plotted to destroy them. Once again, God rescued his people through feasting.

When we turn to the New Testament, we find Jesus fasting in the wilderness and being tempted by the enemy to turn stones into bread. Jesus's response is telling: "Man shall not live on bread alone, but on every word that proceeds out of the mouth of God" (Matt. 4:4). This kind of language was familiar to the Jewish people. Jeremiah had said, "Your words were found and I ate them, and Your words became for me a joy and the delight of my heart" (Jer. 15:16). Ezekiel had a vision in which he was handed a scroll of God's Word and told that he should take and eat it (see Ezek. 3:3). A psalmist wrote that God's Word was sweeter to him than honey from the honeycomb (see Ps. 119:103). The food of our souls is the Word that God gives us to consume.

Jesus goes beyond this. At the ancient Passover meal on the night he was betrayed, Jesus did something radical. Toward the end of the meal, he took the bread and, after offering thanks, broke it and gave it to his disciples, saying, "Take and eat. This is my body, which is broken for you." Then, at the end of the meal, he took the cup—the cup of blessing—and said, "This cup is the new covenant in my blood, which is shed for you and for many for the remission of sins. Drink from it, all of you . . . and this do in remembrance of me." Jesus took the ancient Passover Supper—his last supper with his disciples before he went to the cross—and turned it into the Lord's Supper, in which he offers himself to us as true food and true drink. In that moment, the new covenant became a reality, and those who ate that meal confessed to being members of Jesus's new creation people.

Jesus himself said that we are to eat his flesh and drink his blood (see John 6:53). His words are hard to understand, and this brings us right back to the ancient meaning of that term *sacrament*—a mystery. How is it that we can feast on Christ himself as he offers himself to us in the Lord's Supper?

Through the centuries, Christians have offered a variety of explanations for the "how" of this great mystery. This little chapter isn't long enough to even begin to scratch the surface of those views—whole libraries are written on the subject. Instead, I'd like us to come back to the basic idea of what a sacrament is: God's speaking to us in a sign and applying to us, through the Holy Spirit, Jesus's work and presence. Does that answer every question or satisfy all curiosity? Definitely not. Nor would I suggest that investigations into this mystery are unimportant—they're very important! The simple reality, though, if we may return to a childlike faith, is that Christ is offered to you as your true food and your true drink. This happens through the power of the Holy Spirit in the worship of God's people as they gather around the table of the Lord in his presence. I need participation a lot more than I need explanation. I need to receive far more than I need to be informed.

Let's consider some insights from the Westminster Confession of Faith that are vital for helping us to understand what happens in the Lord's Supper.[3]

The Perpetual Remembrance of the Sacrifice of Our Lord Jesus in His Death

In the Lord's Supper, we *remember* Jesus's death for us. We are a forgetful people—spiritual amnesiacs who need to be reminded of the goodness of God and the beauty of the gospel. The Lord's Supper keeps constantly before our eyes his promise about the sufficiency of his death on our behalf. Christ offered himself once and for all on the cross to forgive us our sins—given our continued struggles with sin, we need to be reminded of this great truth on a daily basis. This means, as well, that the Lord's Supper is not a reward for good behavior but instead a reminder of how deep our need is. When I come to the feast of faith at the Lord's Table, I come not because I think I have done well but because I know he has done all things well. He alone is my righteousness.

The Sealing All Benefits of Jesus's Sacrifice unto True Believers

At the Lord's Supper we have sealed to us all the benefits that are in our relationship with Jesus Christ. In a sense, the

---

3. See the Westminster Confession of Faith, chapter 29.

Lord's Supper calls us to explore the treasure house of God's many graces in our lives. The Savior who offered himself once and for all for our sins offers himself to us continually at the table. In this act, Jesus Christ brings us into his presence and brings his presence into us in such a way that all the benefits that he has procured for us in the cross are made our own in our experience.

True Believers' Spiritual Nourishment and Growth in Him

All Christians acknowledge that we need to grow spiritually. Many people encourage growth through prayer and Bible study and church attendance. All these are, of course, very important. I'm always amazed, however, when people leave out the Lord's Supper as a means of growth in grace. The Lord's Supper is a place of spiritual nourishment. Its small portions of wine and bread have within them the capacity to create massive growth. It isn't the size of the serving in the feast that counts; it is the serving of the Savior to our souls that creates the blessing.

We come to this supper and feast on Christ by faith, and in doing this with our brothers and sisters we grow in faith. You may not remember what you had for dinner two weeks ago last Thursday—we forget meals fairly quickly, unless they are spectacular. But we would not forget going hungry. We would not forget the day we did not have enough money to feed ourselves or our families. Hunger stands out. We may not remember every time we come to the Lord's Table, and we may be tempted to think that the bread and the wine don't constitute much of a feast. Yet through these ordinary elements, Christ himself is offered to us. By receiving him, we receive the grace we need in order to grow in faith.

True Believers' Further Engagement in and to All Duties Which They Owe unto Him

The Lord's Supper reminds us that our participation in Christ's body and blood obligates us to follow him. Participating in the Lord's Supper identifies us with Jesus Christ and his people. Unlike baptism, which others perform for our benefit, the Lord's Supper is taken by our own choice. In making the choice, we acknowledge that we belong not to ourselves but to Jesus and that we must respond to our King with joyful obedience—whatever he requires of us.

A Bond and Pledge of Their Communion with Him, and with Each Other

The Lord's Supper speaks to us of our union with Christ and with other believers. Jesus said, "He who eats My flesh and drinks My blood abides in Me, and I in him" (John 6:56). When we partake of this communion with the body and blood of Christ, the great mystery of union with Christ is brought before our hearts and minds again. We are one with Jesus Christ, and our union extends to his entire body, to all believers who are with us at the table, and to those beyond as well. One cannot be united to Jesus and not be united to his people. That is why the Lord's Supper does not belong to a particular denomination or even a single congregation. It is the Lord's Table, not ours. Every member of his family is welcome. We belong to one another, and the Lord's table reminds us of that fact.

In heaven we will experience the fullness of life that is found in the community of the Trinity. This community is imaged in us when we gather and thrive in a community of grace. At the Lord's Table, that community of grace is created and sustained. It is a community of fallen but forgiven people, who prophesy the age to come every time they gather for the feast in this present age. This is not a personal meal but a shared meal. The Trinity shares life with us, and each of us extends to one another the grace that God gave to us all.

The Lord's Supper transcends time. It takes us back to the cross and forward into the eternal life that is ours. "As often as you eat this bread and drink the cup, you proclaim [in the present] the Lord's death [in the past] until He comes [in the future]," Paul wrote (1 Cor. 11:26). The Lord's Supper communicates to us the entire scope of our redemption and invites us to participate now in an age that is yet to come fully into view. The Lord's Supper is the gospel proclaimed in sign language. In the bread that is torn, I see his body broken. In the fire of the wine, I taste the cleansing power of his blood. In the faces of those around me, I find the community for which I was created. In the words of promise that are spoken over the feast, I hear again the message of hope that my soul needs in this dark world.

In addition to understanding how to prepare food beautifully and safely, and how to bring various spices and herbs together to create amazing feasts, every chef must learn that the most important ingredient in every recipe is love. At the Lord's Table, this rule is especially the case. Whatever the quality of the bread or wine on the table, the truth remains that in this Supper, in this Feast of all Feasts, we see the love of God in Jesus Christ offered to us. That love brings us back into contact with the beauty of his sacrifice for us at the cross.

THE FAMILY TABLE

In baptism we enter into God's family, and at the Lord's Table God nourishes our newfound faith. We grow together with other brothers and sisters because Christianity is never practiced in isolation. We are part of God's family, and that family gathers around the family table to hear again the great story of how God in Christ reconciled us to himself. At that table we tell each other the stories of how God has worked in our lives. There we dry each other's tears, pray for one another, and extend to one another the hospitality of the kingdom of heaven. In both baptism and the Lord's Supper, we encounter in beautiful ways the joyful and sacrificial grace of God. These sacraments, then, are not optional extras on a spiritual growth menu. They are the indispensable mysteries of what it means to be a Christian.

FOR REFLECTION OR GROUP DISCUSSION

1. The author describes the sacraments as "divine signage." Discuss the visible aspect of the sacraments of baptism and Communion. What message do the visible, physical elements suggest to you?

2. Signs aren't the thing that they signify, though the language of signs is connected to what they are communicating. How does baptism speak of cleansing? How do eating bread and drinking wine say something about our need for Christ?

3. In addition to cleansing, baptism is a sign of union with another—with Christ and his church. Does that mean that every baptized person, whether an infant or an adult, will turn out to be a faithful Christian? Why or why not?

4. God creates humans "hungry" and sets before us a feast. In what ways does the biblical story of creation, fall, redemption, and consummation revolve around the idea of feasting and banquet?

5. *Sacrament* is an English-language derivative of the Latin *sacramentum*, which is, in turn, a translation of the Greek word for "mystery." In other words, sacraments are a "mystery" that God uses to minister his grace in our lives in a way that can't be fully grasped by our limited understanding. Take a few minutes to describe some of the mystery that surrounds baptism and communion.

6. Take the following words about Communion and discuss together the way in which we can best embrace their truth.

   a. *Remember*
   b. *Sealed*
   c. *Nourished*
   d. *Engage*
   e. *Pledge*

7. As a group, sing "When I Survey the Wondrous Cross" by Isaac Watts.

12

THE BODY OF CHRIST
The Indispensable Community

I will build my church.
—*Jesus Christ*

Wilson!
—*Chuck Noland*, Cast Away

One of my favorite films is the 2000 Robert Zemeckis survival movie *Cast Away*, starring Tom Hanks and Helen Hunt. It's surely the only film in which a volleyball plays a leading character role. Adrift at sea on a rapidly disintegrating handmade raft, Hank's character, Chuck Noland, loses touch with the volleyball, which he's named Wilson, during a last-ditch search for rescue. Here's the moving script from that iconic scene:

Where's Wilson? Where's Wilson? Wilson, where are you? Wilson! Wilson! Wilson!

Wilson! I'm comin'! Wilson! Wilson! Wilson—[gurgling] Wilson! Wilson! Wilson! [gasping, panting] [coughs] Wilson! Wilson! I'm sorry! I'm sorry, Wilson! Wilson, I'm sorry! I'm sorry! Wilson! [sobbing] I can't! Wilson! Wilson! [sobbing loudly] I'm—I'm sorry. I'm sorry. I'm sorry.[1]

Why would a grown man sob when a volleyball floats away from him at sea? Why would he try to rescue the ball? Why would he convulse in anguish over its loss? If you've seen the film, you know the reason why: that volleyball, Wilson, was the only companion the castaway knew. Absent any other humans, he substituted the unreal for the real—he had to do so, because we were created for community. Alone on an island for years, he could not maintain his full humanity apart from a relationship. Some might have thought that his lengthy conversations with a volleyball were proof that he had lost his sanity, but in fact they were the only way for him to maintain his sanity. Why is our need for the interpersonal dimension so deep?

LONGING FOR BELONGING

The incredible reality is that God fashioned us for relationships—and we don't do isolation well. That's why solitary confinement is a punishment. When God created all things, he declared them to be "very good"—with one notable exception: "It is not good for the man to be alone" (Gen. 2:18). In his play *The Cocktail Party*, poet T. S. Eliot wrote, "What is hell? Hell is oneself. Hell is alone."[2] Thankfully God did not

1. "Where's Wilson?" *Cast Away*, directed by Robert Zemeckis (2000; Beverly Hills, CA: Twentieth Century Fox Home Entertainment, 2002), DVD.
2. T. S. Eliot, *The Cocktail Party*, in *The Complete Poems and Plays: 1909–1950* (New York: Harcourt Brace & Company, 1952), 342.

leave Adam in his aloneness but instead brought Adam into a unique relationship with a particular person—Eve, the woman God had created to be his bride. While that's a terrific love story in many ways, it's a lot more than that. In fact, it reveals the eternal purpose for which God sent his Son to die on the cross and rise again.

Paul wrote to the Ephesians that the relationship between a husband and wife is a window into something deeper, more lasting, and even more loving.

> Husbands, love your wives, as Christ loved the church and gave himself up for her, that he might sanctify her, having cleansed her by the washing of water with the word, so that he might present the church to himself in splendor, without spot or wrinkle or any such thing, that she might be holy and without blemish. In the same way husbands should love their wives as their own bodies. He who loves his wife loves himself. For no one ever hated his own flesh, but nourishes and cherishes it, just as Christ does the church, because we are members of his body. "Therefore a man shall leave his father and mother and hold fast to his wife, and the two shall become one flesh." This mystery is profound, and I am saying that it refers to Christ and the church. (Eph. 5:25–32 ESV)

Something even more mysterious than the love between a man and a woman is going on. The bigger story is that Christ gave his life out of love for his bride, the church. Salvation is deeply personal, but it's also deeply interpersonal. Christ died not simply for individuals considered in isolation but for an entire community of people that he called "my church." Paul said that it was for the church that Christ shed his blood (see Acts 20:28), and he went on to write of the church as Christ's "bride," for whom he sacrificially gave his life (see Eph. 5:25–32). I am not personally the bride of Christ, and neither are you; together with all Christians in all times and all places, however, we are part of that glorious community.

The book of Revelation teaches us that history wraps up with a new heaven and new earth—with all things made new, as the church, Jesus's bride, is revealed in pristine splendor. The wedding celebration is massive, as eternity is launched with the most exquisite banquet imaginable.

> "Let us rejoice and be glad and give the glory to Him, for the marriage of the Lamb has come and His bride has made herself ready." It was given to her to clothe herself in fine linen, bright and clean; for the fine linen is the righteous acts of the saints. Then he said to me, "Write, 'Blessed are those who are invited to the marriage supper of the Lamb.'" And he said to me, "These are true words of God." (Rev. 19:7–9)

IT'S NOT ABOUT ME

If we think that the gospel is exclusively about a personal eternal destination, we take the gospel message and twist it into one of our modern idols: the idol of self. This idol distorts our expectations of the church, transforming us from covenant-keeping fellow members of one another into religious consumers looking to find the church with the best products to meet what we perceive to be our spiritual needs. Many churches go right along with this, with the result that the faith is basically "on sale," as the church looks to attract buyers rather than seeking to be a community of disciples that grows disciples.

To escape this consumerist distortion, we have to take

this thing called "church" more seriously. Far from being a choice on a menu of spiritual growth options, the church is in fact the entire context of redemption. History is headed toward the church's revelation, before the watching universe, as the perfect and perfectly beautiful bride of Christ—so we need to make sure that we are included in the building project that Jesus has undertaken. We were made for one another in a community of faith—created for union with Christ and with each other in his body.

For this reason, for as long as I can recall, I have said, "I believe in the church" every Sunday of my life. When we confess the church's great summaries of the faith—its creeds—we say that we believe in the Father and what he's done, the Son and what he's done, and the Spirit and what he's done. But, as magnificent and precious as these truths are, we don't stop there. No; we continue by saying, "I believe in the church." The church is just as much a part of indispensable Christianity as the Father, the Son, and the Holy Spirit are.

WHO NEEDS THE CHURCH?

Not every Christian considers belief in the church—at least as the church is historically considered, as a worshiping, confessing, serving, disciplined community—to be as important as I am arguing. In fact, disregarding the church and dismissing it as irrelevant is fairly fashionable. Criticizing the church is pretty easy, to be honest. I know a lot of people who still have faith in Jesus but have lost faith in the church out of disappointment, pain, and disillusionment.

I know the feeling. In my late teens, I threw in the towel on everything to do with the church. Why? It wasn't that I'd lost my faith in Jesus; in fact, I was operating with a super-spiritual zeal that I interpreted as radical Christianity. In my view, I was rejecting a tired, hypocritical, lukewarm institution in favor of a new, informal, powerful, totally dedicated approach to faith. Since Jesus condemned the lukewarm church, why shouldn't I? How could I stay a part of something that was so self-evidently compromised? I walked away from the church because I was trying to get closer to Jesus.

But even when we remake our spirituality in totally privatized terms, we continue to crave the good experience of church. Atheist congregations meet on weekends for fellowship, songs, and a talk—a sermon of sorts—because former members of churches know that they need what the faith offered them, even if they no longer believe. Atheist Julian Barnes begins his book *Nothing to Be Frightened Of* by saying, "I don't believe in God, but I miss Him."[3] Still others look for an experience of faith through alternative spiritualities or even entertainment. Maren Morris's country hit "My Church" reflects that reality. In it, Morris clearly articulates what so many people crave: we all need God's grace that is given through the power of the Spirit to take us beyond the grip of our multiple failures and sins. Can we find that somewhere? Sadly, for Morris the answer is found not in *the* church but in *her* church, under the care of Pastor Hank Williams, with choir director Johnny Cash doing ministry in the sanctuary of her car as it speeds down the highway with its radio turned up loud.[4] It's a spiritual experience that you may have enjoyed as well, even if your musical denomination differs from hers.

I want Maren Morris to be able to show up in Jesus's church and get the full treatment of the great news of the gospel, because one of the hallmarks of Jesus's church is that it

3. Julian Barnes, *Nothing to Be Frightened Of* (2008; repr., London: Vintage, 2009), 1.

4. See Maren Morris, vocalist, "My Church," by Maren Morris and busbee, track 3 on *Hero*, Columbia Nashville, 2016.

keeps telling us the story of his redeeming love, over and over again, through songs, service, sermons, studies, and prayers. I want everyone to experience the wonder of that grace. Then I want them to encounter something else—a grace that flows from the gospel as well: the committed community of believers loving each other and their neighbors in authentic faith. That takes the church—precisely because it's the church that embodies the message of Jesus, giving it flesh and bones.

BODYBUILDING 101

This flesh-and-bones dimension of Christian faith is why Paul calls the church "the body of Christ." This body, the church, is part of indispensable Christianity. Paul wrote to the badly divided and hurting church at Corinth, telling them that despite the mess they were in they were nonetheless Christ's body. Christ is the Head and each Christian a "member" of the body—all valuable, all different, all joined together through the Holy Spirit for the common flourishing of that community and the spread of the good news (see 1 Cor. 12:12–31). Each and every Christian is a member of the body and is necessary for the health and well-being of the whole. This results not only in the health of the church but also in opportunities for non-Christians to see Jesus at work. Just as the Spirit formed Jesus's physical body in the womb of Mary, the Spirit forms us into the body Jesus uses to continue his ministry before a watching world.

> For even as the body is one and yet has many members, and all the members of the body, though they are many, are one body, so also is Christ. For by one Spirit we were all baptized into one body, whether Jews or Greeks, whether slaves or free, and we were all made to drink of one Spirit.

. . . Now you are Christ's body, and individually members of it. (1 Cor. 12:12–13, 27)

Of course, some people may be tempted to see themselves as superior to others—as not needing any connection beyond their inner circle. That's one problem that keeps us from the church: even if we recognize the contribution we could make, we don't think that we need anyone else's gifts. Spiritually self-contained and self-sufficient, we isolate ourselves from the potential demands and pain that commitment to other broken people will surely mean. Still others suffer from a kind of spiritual low self-esteem, isolating themselves from others because, as they look at their lives—their own pain, woundedness, and weakness—they wrongly conclude that they have nothing to offer others. Paul speaks to both kinds of people We all need one another. No one can say, "I don't need you" to another Christian; and by the same token, no one can conclude, "No one needs me."

For the body does not consist of one member but of many. If the foot should say, "Because I am not a hand, I do not belong to the body," that would not make it any less a part of the body. And if the ear should say, "Because I am not an eye, I do not belong to the body," that would not make it any less a part of the body. If the whole body were an eye, where would be the sense of hearing? If the whole body were an ear, where would be the sense of smell? But as it is, God arranged the members in the body, each one of them, as he chose. If all were a single member, where would the body be? As it is, there are many parts, yet one body.

The eye cannot say to the hand, "I have no need of you," nor again the head to the feet, "I have no need of you." (1 Cor. 12:14–21 ESV)

One Sunday morning, I was greeting people as they arrived for the worship service when a newcomer responded to my welcome with one of the strangest things I've ever heard. "I'm an eye," he said, shaking my hand. Here was a person with a clear idea of what part of the body of Christ he was—and it seemed a tad arrogant as well. He was announcing that we'd better take his insights seriously, as though he were a seer—a prophet of sorts. Now, eyes are lovely and beautiful—as long as they're where they're supposed to be! When he said, "I'm an eye," all I could think of was a cow's eye on a dissection tray in my high school biology class—not a pretty sight! Disconnected from its living context, it was a source of disgusted squeals from the girls in the class and gruesome jokes from the boys. I hate to admit this, but when he said, "I'm an eye" and that image raced through my memory, I blurted out to him, "Find a face!" That was the only time he visited the church.

I'm so sorry I was that insensitive. The truth is that, however great or small our part may be, we are all loved by Jesus and joined through his Spirit to one another in his church. We all need to "find the face" where we belong and shine in the purpose of God.

THE FRIENDS AND FAMILY YOU DIDN'T CHOOSE

The global reality of the church is also expressed in smaller ways. The body functions together in the service of its members and of the world. All believers—from the smallest infant to the most senior saint, from the newest believer to the most mature disciple, from the hurting brothers and sisters to the rejoicing ones—are joined together in mutual love, which is seen in their need of one another, their service to one another, and their encouragement of one another. One mark of authentic spiritual maturity is an awareness that there isn't a single believer who isn't a gift of God's grace to us and that we must welcome them all.

Theologian Stanley Hauerwas notes, "Whatever it means to be a Christian, it at least involves the discovery of friends you did not know you had."[5] Those friends are going to shock you. You're going to find yourself loving people who are very different from you. That's why "the church" can be tough at times. The church isn't an aggregation of people who gather for an event on a Sunday morning and then disperse into the mist of the week; the church is a congregation of the committed, who are very different from one another—racially, economically, politically, generationally, and nationally. That's what makes the church beautiful! The body of Jesus is made up of all kinds of people, from all kinds of places, who are learning what it means to love one another.

As a pastor, I also know that we aren't very good at that sometimes. Loving one another—especially when people are different from us—is tough. It's awkward. We get it wrong and offend one another. We are not well-practiced in love. Yet even these breakdowns can be shakeups that lead us to fresh understandings of grace and hope. This is why Roman Catholic priest and teacher Henri Nouwen reminds us, "Forgiveness is the name of love practiced among people who love poorly. The hard truth is that all people love poorly. We need to forgive and be forgiven every day, every hour increasingly. That is the great work of love among the fellowship of the weak."[6] Being critical of the church? That's easy. We're

5. Stanley Hauerwas, *Hannah's Child: A Theologian's Memoir* (Grand Rapids: Eerdmans, 2010), 228.

6. Henri J. M. Nouwen, quoted in Earl Henslin, *This is Your Brain in Love: New Scientific Breakthroughs for a More Passionate and Emotionally*

weak. We're a mess—yet it's exactly in the middle of the mess that we discover the shape of love.

ACROSS THE YEARS AND OCEANS

This "big-tent" approach to the body of Christ has an ancient name: *catholicity*. While you may immediately think of the Roman Catholic Church, this is a word that all Christians can use to describe our belief in the body of Christ. Cyril, the bishop of Jerusalem in AD 350, described *catholicity* as follows:

> [The church] is called Catholic then because it extends over all the world, from one end of the earth to the other; and because it teaches universally and completely one and all the doctrines which ought to come to men's knowledge, concerning things both visible and invisible, heavenly and earthly; and because it brings into subjection to godliness the whole race of mankind, governors and governed, learned and unlearned; and because it universally treats and heals the whole class of sins, which are committed by soul or body, and possesses in itself every form of virtue which is named, both in deeds and words, and in every kind of spiritual gifts.[7]

If we take this ancient counsel to heart, we can note some truths, which are important to recall, about what it means for us to be part of the church catholic.

Healthy Marriage (Nashville: Thomas Nelson, 2009), 170.

7. Lecture XVIII of "The Catechetical Lectures of S. Cyril, Archbishop of Jerusalem," in *S. Cyril of Jerusalem; S. Gregory Nazianzen, A Select Library of Nicene and Post-Nicene Fathers of the Christian Church*, 2nd ser., ed. Philip Schaff and Henry Wace, vol. 7 (New York, 1894), 139–40.

- The church isn't confined to a nation or ethnicity. The church is global—it includes all people who believe, in all places and all times.
- The church teaches the whole truth—not just the emphases of a particular time or place or "special truths" that only certain people "get" (in fact, this is the very definition of a sect—the opposite of a church). The church teaches the "whole purpose of God" (Acts 20:27) and helps people to keep growing in their walk with God.
- The church is sociologically universal—it embraces all people regardless of their ethnicity, social position, gender, or anything else that could be a means of creating division. The church is called to be a visible demonstration of the unity that Christ will bring about when he returns.
- The church is pastorally holistic, in that it brings healing grace, through the gospel and the sacraments, to every kind of sin; cultivates all the virtues; and cherishes every spiritual gift.

JESUS CAME TO BUILD HIS CHURCH

The church is so important that Jesus made it a central aspect of his saving mission. "I will build my church," he said, "and the gates of hell shall not prevail against it" (Matt. 16:18 ESV). John Stott wrote, "If the church was worth his blood, is it not worth our labor?"[8] Jesus is under no illusions about the church as it exists on earth; as do each of us personally, the church as a congregation is still sinful and fails in many ways.

8. John R. W. Stott, *The Cross of Christ*, 20th anniv. ed. (Downers Grove, IL: InterVarsity Press, 2006), 178.

Yet our shared destiny as the beautiful bride of Christ is sure, and this hope offers us great encouragement while we deal with our present and very deep failures and flaws. There's an old proverb that warns us about looking for a "perfect church": if you find one, don't join it—because that'll ruin it for sure!

I am so thankful that my parents raised me in the church. One gift of such an upbringing is the incomparably meaningful truth that is contained in the church's hymns. One of my favorite hymns celebrates the truth that Jesus created the church to be his bride, that he died to secure her in his love, and that he will perfect her in beauty. "The Church's One Foundation" is a great way for us to close out this chapter as we think deeply about the grace that God gives us as his people, the church.

> The Church's One Foundation is Jesus Christ her Lord,
> She is his new creation by water and the word:
> From heaven he came and sought her to be his holy Bride,
> With his own blood he bought her and for her life he died.
>
> Elect from every nation, yet one o'er all the earth
> Her charter of salvation: one Lord, one faith, one birth.
> One holy name she blesses, partakes one holy food
> And to one hope she presses with every grace endued.
>
> Though with a scornful wonder men see her sore oppressed,
> By schisms rent asunder, by heresies distressed:
> Yet saints their watch are keeping, their cry goes up, "How
>   long?"
> And soon the night of weeping shall be the morn of song!
>
> 'Mid toil and tribulation and tumult of her war,
> She waits the consummation of peace forevermore,

When with the vision glorious her longing eyes are blessed
And the great Church victorious shall be the Church at rest.[9]

FOR REFLECTION OR GROUP DISCUSSION

1. In what ways does our craving for relationship and community, and the pain that we feel in isolation, reflect the fact that we are made in the image of God?

2. Salvation is deeply personal, but it is also deeply interpersonal. In what ways does a church community teach us to deny consumerism in regard to God and to embrace being disciples?

3. The church is called "the body of Christ," and each believer is a "member" of that body. Both pride ("I don't need you!") and dismay ("I have nothing to offer") can rob us of our participation in the body of Christ. Which of the two is more likely to challenge you, and why? What will you do about that challenge?

4. List some reasons that people are abandoning the church today.

5. Does Jesus abandon his church? How does the image of the church as Christ's bride impact your view of the church?

6. Discuss this quote from Henri Nouwen and how we learn to practice forgiveness: "Forgiveness is the name of love practiced among people who love poorly. The hard truth is that all people love poorly. We need to forgive and be forgiven every day, every hour increasingly. That is the great work of love among the fellowship of the weak."

7. What do we mean when we say, "I believe in the Holy Catholic Church"? Make special note of the five

9. Samuel John Stone, "The Church's One Foundation," 1866.

characteristics of what *catholic* really means, as described by St. Cyril of Jerusalem.

8. As a group, sing "The Church's One Foundation" by Samuel John Stone.

13

KNOWING GOD

The Indispensable Pursuit

So let us know, let us press on to know the Lord.
—Hosea the Prophet

I still haven't found what I'm looking for.
—Song by U2

FOMO is a *thing*. It feeds on our insecurities, haunting us just when we thought we were doing okay. What is it? It's *fear of missing out*. I'm cursed with it in spades—especially when it comes to information. I just *know* that I'll make a total fool of myself if I open my mouth, or write a sentence, and show how much I don't know. Paralyzed by the fear of what I've missed—what a terrible way to live! Is there an escape from my own personal information-age FOMO prison?

FOMO about God would have to be the ultimate version of this affliction. We'd be constantly trying to make sure we were mastering the information about him and regretting deeply anything we had overlooked. It would be a life of fearful uncertainty. If that were the case, we would live in a perpetual state of joyless anxiety about the God who is love. That makes no sense at all!

CELEBRATE FOMO

What if we *celebrated* that we don't know as much about God as we think we're supposed to know? What if we simply acknowledged that, when it comes to God, there are no "experts"—that all the shepherds are also sheep; that all the instructors are students; and that, however much we think we know, there's an eternity's worth of material to investigate . . . and that we haven't even scratched the surface? What if when it came to the knowledge of God, we banished FOMO forever by simply admitting, "Yes, I really don't know that much, but I do love learning. Bring it!" That would be healthy, because it's in line with Paul's view.

> We know that we all have knowledge. Knowledge makes arrogant, but love edifies. If anyone supposes that he knows anything, he has not yet known as he ought to know; but if anyone loves God, he is known by Him. (1 Cor. 8:1–3)

We need to remember that, even if we were Mensa-level geniuses in Scripture, we would still be mere gnats in our understanding of God. An old Latin phrase expresses this well: *finitum non capex infiniti*—"the finite cannot fathom the infinite." We may know God truly, but we can never know him exhaustively. Henri Nouwen wisely observed, "Spiritual formation begins with the gradual and often painful discovery of God's incomprehensibility. . . . We might be competent in many subjects, but we cannot become an expert in the things of God."[1]

When I was traveling from the United States to Europe on one occasion, I made the mistake of bringing what I thought was an electric current transformer plug for my razor, when it was in fact a mere plug adapter. The current in the United Kingdom is set at 220 volts, while it's set at 110 volts in the United States. You can guess what happened. When I plugged in my electric razor, it ran really, really well . . . for about fifteen seconds.[2] Then it exploded, leaving me a smoldering mess to clean up.

I'm pretty sure that that's exactly what would happen if we ever got a full-tilt plug-in to the wisdom and knowledge of God. We'd be bright-eyed with wonder for a few seconds, and then—poof!—we'd be toast. Thankfully, God gives us the immense and rich gift of the Scriptures and the presence of the Holy Spirit to guide us into the truth; but even so, we are aware of persistent questions that we wish God would answer and, no matter how much we study, a persistent nagging in our souls that tells us we have not yet adequately explored the depths of God's beauty.

It's not as though we don't "know God"—we do. Yet we are also aware that we do not know him as well as we might and as well as we wish we did. We know there is more. This is why the Hebrew prophet Hosea called God's people to both "know" and to "press on to the know the LORD" (Hos. 6:3). Hosea says that while we do know God, we have so much more of him to discover and love. We must keep moving forward with grateful hearts into the knowledge of God.

1. Henri Nouwen, *Spiritual Formation: Following the Movements of the Spirit* (San Francisco: HarperOne, 2010), 3.
2. And I do mean *really* well—it sounded like a jet turbine engine was powering up.

One of the greatest early church leaders, St. Irenaeus, pointed out that whatever we think we now know of God is only by way of introduction—that we will always need deeper instruction. He wrote,

> If . . . there are some things only God knows, . . . why should we complain if, in regard to those things which we investigate in the Scriptures . . . , we are able . . . to explain only some of them, while we must leave the rest in the hands of God—and that not only in the present world but also in that which is to come—so that God will forever teach and human beings will forever learn the things God teaches? . . . It encourages us always to hope confidently that we will always receive more and more from God and learn from him, since he is good and has boundless riches, an unending kingdom, and inexhaustible instruction.[3]

For Irenaeus, humankind will ever have more of God to learn, and God will ever have more of himself to offer us. In a sense, that's what eternity is for!

MOVING FORWARD AS DISCIPLES

Far from producing spiritual apathy in us, the impossibly immense knowledge of God inspires in us the same kind of wonder and passion that mountaineers experience in the face of Everest. In *The Last Battle*, the epic conclusion to C. S. Lewis's Chronicles of Narnia, Queen Lucy observes, "A stable once had something inside it that was bigger than our whole

---

3. James R. Peyton Jr., *Irenaeus on the Christian Faith: A Condensation of Against Heresies* (Eugene, OR: Wipf & Stock, 2011), 50.

world."[4] God's vast and boundless beauty is always accompanied by his matchless grace, which invites us to go deep and high and wide and long in our pursuit of him. The manger in Bethlehem testifies to God's desire to contract himself to our space and be among us—*to be known.* The knowledge of God is a gift given by God himself—Jesus's incarnation reveals the Father, as do the Scriptures and the Spirit, who works in our lives to deepen our love for God and our knowledge of his love for us.

This is why Paul's prayers for the church at Ephesus are so important. He begins by praying that God will give them

> the spirit of wisdom and revelation in the knowledge of him: the eyes of [their] understanding being enlightened; that [they] may know what is the hope of his calling, and what the riches of the glory of his inheritance in the saints, and what is the exceeding greatness of his power. (Eph. 1:17–19 KJV)

As astonishing as that prayer is, Paul is just warming up. He then writes that he asks the Father

> that He would grant you, according to the riches of His glory, to be strengthened with power through His Spirit in the inner man, so that Christ may dwell in your hearts through faith; and that you, being rooted and grounded in love, may be able to comprehend with all the saints what is the breadth and length and height and depth, and to know the love of Christ which surpasses knowledge, that you may be filled up to all the fullness of God. (Eph. 3:16–19)

4. C. S. Lewis, *The Last Battle* (repr., New York: Collier Books, 1970), 141–42.

Paul prays that God's people will know something beyond knowing—the love of God that "surpasses" knowledge. He prays that we will enter into a relationship with God that transcends every dimension of our existence. He prays that we will do this with others, because it cannot be done on our own. He prays that we will grow in this relationship and will be rooted deeply in the soil of God's unchanging, sacrificial love for us.

These apostolic prayers encourage us to rejoice in rather than to fear our lack of knowledge. Let's take them as the instruction we need in order to walk with humble reliance on the grace of a God who continually invites us into a deeper relationship with himself. We are committed to growing in our faith, following after Christ, and embracing our God-ordained destiny to be conformed to his image (see Rom. 8:29).

This process of transformation is called *sanctification*. While justification is a once-and-for-all declaration that God makes about us, based exclusively on Jesus's finished work on the cross, sanctification is God's ongoing work in us through the means of grace (prayer, sacraments, and Scripture received in the community of faith called the church) that leads to our growth in authentic holiness and to a life that is characterized by love. Sanctification works out in our lives the implications of justification. A passage in Ephesians 2, which is located directly between Paul's two prayers for the church, presents a classic summary of this truth.

> By grace you have been saved through faith; and that not of yourselves, it is the gift of God; not as a result of works, so that no one may boast. For we are His workmanship, created in Christ Jesus for good works, which God prepared beforehand so that we would walk in them. (Eph. 2:8–10)

We don't work to achieve salvation. Instead, we freely receive it. We can't earn it by working, but we receive it through believing. Having been saved by grace through faith, we discover that we are God's handiwork, fashioned by him for good works he has ordained and for a life of joyful obedience to God. These good works stand in contrast to any works that we thought would save us—our boast-inducing self-salvation efforts appealed to our own tattered righteousness as the basis of our relationship with God (a possibility that the cross of Christ demolishes), while these new "good works" are the thankful offering of the justified who live to serve God in love. We are not saved by any of our works, but we are saved *for* good works that God gives us to do. Richard Sibbes put it this way: "By grace we are what we are in justification, and work what we work in sanctification."[5]

We don't spend the rest of our lives seeking to alleviate suffering, love our neighbors, develop and deploy our gifts, close the door on temptations, deny sin access to our minds, hearts, and bodies, and dedicate our mouths, eyes, hands, and feet to God's will because we are trying to win God's approval and acceptance. Never! We know that he delights in us and tenderly cares for us; and the cross is the revelation of his love. "God demonstrates His own love toward us, in that while we were yet sinners, Christ died for us" (Rom. 5:8). We seek to live holy lives of love, because our destiny is to be conformed to the image of Christ and because we long for his beauty to be seen in and through us. We rest in the truth of the gospel—that we are once and for all made right with God by grace. We rejoice in the truth that the God who accepts us as we are, on the basis of Christ's righteousness,

5. Alexander Balloch Grosart, ed., *The Complete Works of Richard Sibbes, D. D.* (Edinburgh, 1863) 6:245.

loves us too much to leave us as we are and will transform us by his grace.

Let's look at a few ways in which God works to bring our lives more and more into conformity with the life of Jesus.

LOVE

"We love him because he first loved us," wrote the apostle John. God has taken the initiative in renewing humankind's broken bond with himself and one another by acting in love toward his enemies: "While we were enemies we were reconciled to God through the death of His Son" (Rom. 5:10). Amazingly, the love of God embraces not only those who are "near and dear" but those who openly oppose him. We might die for our families because we love them, and a soldier might die for his country because he loves it—but who dies in love for his sworn enemy?

In *The Magnificent Defeat*, Frederick Buechner writes,

The love for equals is a human thing—of friend for friend, brother for brother. It is to love what is loving and lovely. The world smiles.

The love for the less fortunate is a beautiful thing—the love for those who suffer, for those who are poor, the sick, the failures, the unlovely. This is compassion, and it touches the heart of the world.

The love for the more fortunate is a rare thing—to love those who succeed where we fail, to rejoice without envy with those who rejoice, the love of the poor for the rich, of the black man for the white man. The world is always bewildered by its saints.

And then there is the love for the enemy—love for the one who does not love you but mocks, threatens, and inflicts pain. The tortured's love for the torturer. This is God's love. It conquers the world.[6]

What does sanctification look like? It looks like love— God's love being received with joy and offered in sacrifice. Paul is clear that if he had "all knowledge" (no FOMO there!) but did not have love, he would be nothing but "a noisy gong or a clanging cymbal" (see 1 Cor. 13:1–3). In Romans he says that all God's commandments are summed up by love:

> For this, "You shall not commit adultery, You shall not murder, You shall not steal, You shall not covet," and if there is any other commandment, it is summed up in this saying, "You shall love your neighbor as yourself." Love does no wrong to a neighbor; therefore love is the fulfillment of the law. (Rom. 13:9–10)

Two friends of mine were on a mission trip in a major Asian city when they were approached by a prostitute offering her services. To the shock of one of the men, the other asked, "How much?" When she gave him the price, he looked at her and said, "That's not enough. You're worth far more . . . infinitely more. Your body and soul are loved by Jesus, who gave his life for you." This woman who had known only violent oppression at the hands of men heard about the perfectly loving man who gave up his life for her. She was changed by love.

We saw in chapter 7 that God works his love for his enemies into the life of the Christian as well. True holiness offers a life in service, love, and forgiveness even for

---

6. Frederick Buechner, *The Magnificent Defeat* (repr., San Francisco: HarperSanFrancisco, 1985), 105.

one's enemies—blessing others when cursing and bitterness might be expected. Church history is filled with exploits of love. Many who despise the church want to highlight our sins and failures—and we confess that they are many. Yet it is equally true that many have given faithful witness to God's love, and sacrificially so—and it is toward this kind of love that the Spirit leads us so that we might "become conformed to the image of His Son" (Rom. 8:29), who loved us from the cross, redeeming and forgiving even those who nailed him to it.

GATHERED WORSHIP

In chapter 12, I described the grace and beauty of being part of God's covenant family. I want to reiterate the point here, because our growth in the knowledge of God takes place within a community.

Some of my friends have abandoned the church in order to pursue private paths to spiritual vitality. I once asked one of these friends if he actually believed the Bible. An enthusiastic, gregarious sort, he joyfully responded, "I believe it all, from Genesis to Maps!"

After we laughed together, I asked him if he believed the table of contents.

"What do you mean?"

"Well," I said, "you claim to believe the Bible, and I am so glad you do. It has a table of contents page—a list of the books that are received as Scripture. Do you think the contents page is correct?"

He looked at me a little quizzically and answered, "I guess I do."

"Great!" I answered. "Now, tell me—where does that page come from? Who wrote that page? Who recognized what books should end up on that page so that you even have a Bible?"

He pondered that and then said, "The church." He got that right!

"Look," I told him, "you don't want to be part of the church. You want Christianity to look like a personal walk with Jesus, in which you live on your own with your Bible and the Spirit but without the hassle of other people and their crazy problems—but the Bible that you want to base this on was given in and to a community of people, not an isolated individual. It's an 'us' document before it's a 'you' document."

The church is a mess? Yes; guilty as charged—especially me. Yet when I gather with other messed-up people to sit under the Scriptures and at the Lord's Table, I discover that this is the family in which I am called to grow up. Together we learn the art of forgiveness and the joy of service, and together we retune our hearts and voices for the worship of heaven. Sunday morning is a preview of coming attractions: the saints gathered before the throne of God and, together with the angels and archangels, giving glory to Christ, the Lamb of God.

Gathering for worship is the single most radical act that any Christian can make today. We live in an anti-God, anti-church, anti-Christ culture of death, shame, and narcissistic self-love, in which secularist fundamentalism demands that you stay in bed, chill, keep quiet, and find fulfillment in pursuing your personal dreams. In this culture, it is a radical act to respond to God's call to rise from mere individualism or from the boundaries of family and to identify in public with the church of history, the church of heaven, and the church right now. It is radical to offer oneself in sacrifice to the One who sacrificed all on the cross; to publicly acknowledge personal and institutional sin and one's need for forgiveness, instruction, spiritual nourishment, and renewal; to confess in public with others the truth of the ancient faith that is so vehemently despised.

You may find aspects of worship boring. You may not like shared prayers and some of the songs, and the sermon may be a sleeper on some days; you may prefer the quiet of home to the bustling of late-arriving, frazzled families who have been hustling just to get there at all; you may not like some of the practices; you may not seem to relate to some of the people there, because of your age or your race or your politics, or whatever; you may reason that if you don't participate, no one will ask you to give any money; you may not imagine that anything special is going on in that worship service. You'd be wrong. You need those people, and they need you. Moreover, the angels are present in worship; Jesus is present in worship. The keeping of those old musty traditions of gathered worship on the Lord's Day is not "the worship of ashes but the preservation of a fire."[7] In gathered worship, we ascend to heaven and join the whole host of heaven in magnifying the Lord.

Annie Dillard is surely correct when she writes,

> On the whole, I do not find Christians, outside of the catacombs, sufficiently sensible of conditions. Does anyone have the foggiest idea what sort of power we so blithely invoke? Or, as I suspect, does no one believe a word of it? The churches are children playing on the floor with their chemistry sets, mixing up a batch of TNT to kill a Sunday morning. . . . Ushers should issue life preservers and signal flares; they should lash us to our pews. For the sleeping

---

7. Gustav Mahler . . . perhaps. There is no verifiable source for this, and it is at best an English translation of Mahler's own German paraphrase of an aphorism.

god may wake someday and take offense, or the waking god may draw us out to where we can never return.[8]

If we want to get serious about sanctification, we need to get serious about life in the church. What we are part of is more important than the part that we play. We grow together in the family of faith. Join me.

CATECHESIS

"Cata-*what?*" *Catechesis* is a sweet word that Luke uses in the first part of his gospel. It means "instruction." It's also where we get the more contemporary word *catechism*. Luke wrote, "It seemed fitting for me . . . , having investigated everything carefully from the beginning, to write it out for you in consecutive order . . . so that you may know the exact truth about the things you have been taught" (Luke 1:3–4). He wrote his gospel to help people who were already believers to keep growing in their faith. He knew they had been "taught" (catechized), but there was more—much more—for them to learn.

Catechizing in the faith is as essential now as it was in Luke's day—that is why he wrote his gospel and why we need to study the Scriptures. Catechisms are brief summaries of the faith in question-and-answer format. They help us to think about and retain the big issues of our faith. Many people have given up on "catechizing," even though the ancient Christians did it to establish people in the faith. The Reformers faced the same problem in their day and wrote new catechisms to help their generation to better grasp the basics of the faith.

8. Annie Dillard, *Teaching a Stone to Talk: Expeditions and Encounters* (New York: Harper & Row, 1982), 58.

The great news is that those Reformation-era catechisms still inspire and instruct today, and some "modern-language" approaches also help people to learn the vocabulary of grace. Whether one uses the Westminster Shorter Catechism, the Heidelberg Catechism, or the recently published New City Catechism, the truths in these tidy and pithy summaries can help us to "retain the standard of sound words" we have inherited from the apostles (2 Tim. 1:13).

SUFFERING

I hate to mention this, but growing in Christ involves suffering with Christ and for Christ. The life of faith is a life of suffering, and we're just not very comfortable with that in our highly polished, success-driven North American version of Christianity. In fact, many Christian leaders teach that suffering—whether it is physical, psychological, financial, or spiritual—has no place in a Christian life; if we have enough faith, all our troubles will cease. This is nonsense, as both Scripture and history make clear. In fact, it takes amazing faith to walk through suffering and to recognize in it an offering we can give to God.

Paul wrote, "The Spirit Himself testifies with our spirit that we are children of God . . . if indeed we suffer with Him so that we may also be glorified with Him" (Rom. 8:16–17). There's no glory in the end without a cross in the meantime. Being Jesus's disciples means taking seriously his call to "take up [your] cross daily and follow [Him]" (Luke 9:23). Peter wrote,

> Beloved, do not be surprised at the fiery ordeal among you, which comes upon you for your testing, as though some strange thing were happening to you; but to the degree

that you share the sufferings of Christ, keep on rejoicing, so that also at the revelation of His glory you may rejoice with exultation. (1 Peter 4:12–13)

The various forms that suffering takes, from illness to persecution to death, have a common bond—they are sent by the devil to shake our faith in God's goodness.

In 2 Corinthians 12:7–10, we see that when Paul faced unrelenting suffering, he prayed for deliverance. Just like us, he wanted out of his suffering; he wanted the "messenger of Satan" sent to afflict him to be banished from his experience. To that desire, God—strangely—said, "No." In God's refusal, Paul discovered God's mercy. He discovered something even greater than freedom from suffering: the sustaining grace of God that takes our weaknesses and shows Christ's power through them. He discovered that his torment threw him down in fresh dependence on God's strength. He discovered that suffering was part of his worship and service to God. Our suffering is not random and meaningless but is instead an offering that we make to Christ, who suffered for us; and when we suffer we enter the "fellowship of His sufferings, being conformed to His death" (Phil. 3:10).

My friend Phyllis has suffered deeply—and shown grace beautifully. Her daughter gave birth to twin girls, one of whom had very serious birth defects and died after a year of struggle. We gathered at the graveside and committed her to Christ. Not long afterward, Phyllis's daughter was driving home from work late at night when she was struck head-on by the car of an intoxicated driver. She was killed instantly.

Not only had Phyllis lost both a granddaughter and daughter, but she also faced the prospect of raising her surviving granddaughter as her own. We gathered for yet another graveside service. After greeting shocked and saddened mourners back at her home, Phyllis got her coat and prepared to leave.

"Phyllis, where are you headed? Can I go get you something?" I asked.

"I'm going to the jail," she said. "I need to see the driver of that other car and share the gospel with him. I can't think of anyone who more needs to hear about the love of Jesus right now than he does. You just know he has to be in despair. I think he'll listen to me."

I'm sure he did.

The truth is that our suffering and service make the gospel believable and beautiful in a world that's in the deranged pursuit of pleasure and power. The pain of the saints has always done more to open doors for the gospel than any amount of strength and success has. The suffering church—the church of the crucified—is what we are part of, and when it is our time to suffer, we must not lose faith but instead must offer our pain to God in praise and trust.

Of course, we fear suffering. We don't want it. Woody Allen quipped, "It's not that I'm afraid to die. I just don't want to be there when it happens."[9] What do we do when we get the terminal diagnosis from the doctor? How do we face the suffering of those we love and suffer with them in their struggle? We do cry to God for deliverance and mercy—that impulse is right, and sometimes God does indeed vanquish the disease and terminate the terminal. Sometimes God closes the lion's mouth. Not always. Sometimes God answers with just enough grace to sustain us through the next day. If we must face the worst, how should we approach it? Pastor and martyr Dietrich Bonhoeffer, who

9. Woody Allen, *Without Feathers* (repr., New York: Ballantine Books, 1985), 106.

was killed by the Nazis near the end of WWII, prayed as he prepared for execution,

> We call the name of the One before whom the evil in us cringes, before whom fear and anxiety must themselves be afraid, before whom they shake and take flight; the name of the One who alone conquered fear, captured it and led it away in a victory parade, nailed to the cross and banished it to nothingness; the name of the One who is the victory cry of the humanity that is redeemed from the fear of death—Jesus Christ, the one who was crucified and lives. He alone is the Lord of fear; it knows him as its Lord and yields to him alone. Therefore, look to him in your fear. Think about him, place him before your eyes, and call him. Pray to him and believe that he is now with you and helps you. The fear will yield and fade, and you will become free through faith in the strong and living Savior Jesus Christ (Matt. 8:23–27).[10]

THE SHAPE OF SANCTIFICATION

If, while reading this, you're thinking, "Right! I'm going to get better at this Christian thing every day . . ." I need to jump in and burst your bubble. Sanctification doesn't look like that; in fact, it looks more like an increasing awareness of how miserably we fail at being faithful believers—a deepening awareness of our need for daily mercy. Growing in grace doesn't mean that our lives look so much better as much as it means that the cross of Jesus looks so much bigger and more important to us.

10. Dietrich Bonhoeffer, *God Is in the Manger: Reflections on Advent and Christmas* (Louisville: Westminster John Knox Press, 2010), 44.

In her book *Extravagant Grace*, author Barbara Duguid offers one of the most beautiful takes on sanctification that I've ever read. She writes, "If Christians believe that they can actually live up to God's standard and should be achieving that goal better and better each day, then one of two things will happen in the face of the stubborn reality of our hearts. Either we must rewrite God's standards downward into something more achievable . . . or, if we retain the searching intensity of biblical truth, we assume that God is very disappointed in us."[11]

The gospel refuses to lessen the demands of the law; instead, it offers a Savior who meets those demands perfectly on our behalf. The gospel reveals a God who treasures and loves us so much that he would give himself for us and to us—not a Grumpy Cat deity who looks on us with divine displeasure. Duguid gathers up this gospel perspective and offers us the truth about God's grace in sanctification: we discover in the gospel "the grace to find tremendous joy and delight in the Lord in spite of mountains of sin that don't respond to our greatest efforts. Many Christians have never heard of grace that is sufficient to survive brutal failure in our performance and nonetheless enables us to find deep joy and peace in the righteousness of Christ."[12]

God could have made us instantly perfect when he saved us. He didn't. I wish he had. Instead, he is "bringing many sons to glory" (Heb. 2:10) through many—often strange—dealings and graces in our union with Christ.

It is true that one day we will be perfect. Paul wrote that he was "confident of this very thing, that He who began a good work in you will perfect it until the day of Christ Jesus"

---

11. Barbara R. Duguid, *Extravagant Grace: God's Glory Displayed in Our Weakness* (Phillipsburg, NJ: P&R Publishing, 2013), 125–26.

12. Duguid, 126.

(Phil. 1:6) and that at the culmination of God's restorative work in our lives we will be "conformed to the image of His Son" (Rom. 8:29). That future day, for which we wait in biblical hope, is a certain reality, even if it is an uncertain day on our calendars. Until that day dawns, we will keep singing of the "sweet sound" of the amazing grace that saves "wretches" like you and me. We will keep looking away from ourselves and unto Christ as our only righteousness. We will keep walking the path of love in the strength that the Savior supplies, "through many dangers, toils, and snares."[13] We will keep trusting in God's own infallible Word, which is inspired by the same Spirit who beckons us forward in our journey toward our inheritance.

You see, even if we do not know God exhaustively, we can and do know him truly. "Knowing God," said Jesus, "is eternal life" (see John 17:3). This "knowing" isn't confined to an intellectual comprehension of what God is; it's a relational joining to who God is. In the Father's embrace, which is given to us in Jesus and applied to us by the Spirit, we find our heart's true home, the greatest intellectual adventure possible, and the hope of life that transcends our current brokenness. On our journey, God is both the inn at which we rest and our final destination. In this journey with and to God, in the paradox of knowing and still coming to know, I find myself loved in Christ, forgiven in Christ, and destined for Christ.

PRESS ON

Like U2's Bono, I still haven't found what I'm looking for. We are like Abraham and others who through the ages have walked by faith and not by sight, "looking for the city

---

13. John Newton, "Amazing Grace," 1779.

which has foundations, whose architect and builder is God" (Heb. 11:10). We are not home yet. This is life in the meantime, between Jesus's precious words "It is finished" and "It is done." In this journey, we will rejoice, for we have been commended "to God and to the word of his grace, which is able to build you up and to give you the inheritance among all those who are sanctified" (Acts 20:32).

I offer this closing benediction, which has been pronounced for over three thousand years on the people of God, who are saved by grace, gathered to worship, commissioned to serve, sent to love, and led by grace all the way back to the Father's house:

> The LORD bless you, and keep you;
> The LORD make His face shine on you,
> And be gracious to you;
> The LORD lift up His countenance on you,
> And give you peace. (Num. 6:24–26)

In the Name of the Father, the Son, and the Holy Spirit. Amen.

FOR REFLECTION OR GROUP DISCUSSION

1. What does the Latin phrase *finitum non capex infiniti* mean, and how does it apply to our knowledge of God?
2. Read Hosea 6:3 and John 17:3. Eternal life is to "know God"—but will we ever come to exhaust all that is possible to know about God? Should that make us give up on the chase? Why not? How does "loving God" shape our pursuit of him?
3. Read Ephesians 3:14–19, and discuss the following quote from this chapter:

Paul prays that God's people will know something beyond knowing—the love of God that "surpasses" knowledge. He prays that we will enter into a relationship with God that transcends every dimension of our existence. He prays that we will do this with others, because it cannot be done on our own. He prays that we will grow in this relationship and will be rooted deeply in the soil of God's unchanging, sacrificial love for us.

4. Pray this prayer together for one another in your study group.
5. What is sanctification? How does it differ from justification, and why is it so important as we seek to grow in grace?
6. In what ways does having love for others show a growth in holiness?
7. How does gathering with other Christians for worship and studying Scripture help us to grow in our faith and in holiness?
8. How might suffering be part of our growth in grace?
9. As a group, sing "Immortal, Invisible, God Only Wise" by Walter C. Smith.

If I find in myself a desire which no experience
in this world can satisfy, the most probable
explanation is that I was made for another world.
—C. S. Lewis, Mere Christianity

Was this book helpful to you?
Consider writing a review online.
The author appreciates your feedback!

Or write to P&R at editorial@prpbooks.com
with your comments. We'd love to hear from you.